See wha

"The story of her journey was real and raw, and gives me hope for myself as well as other leaders to carry on the work of changing and healing the world."
~ Linda F. Patten, Leadership Trainer for Women Entrepreneurs and Changemakers – President & CEO, Dare2Lead With Linda

"Olivia Parr-Rud is what I call "Smheart." She effectively applies her brilliant, systems-oriented mind and her open, loving heart to the task of proving that Love is the greatest driver of success in business today."
~ Marian Head, author, Revolutionary Agreements:
A Personal Path to Peace on Earth

"Applause for Olivia Parr-Rud using her decades of background in the corporate world as a data and technical expert, keen observer of workforce performance and productivity, and critical thinker about the role of love in effective leadership."
~ Sue Marchner Brightman, Founder, Brightman Glover International Coaching and Consulting in Conscious Business

"Olivia gives you the roadmap to the organization of the future - one where people, profit, and purpose converge into the X-factor of results, revenue, and marketplace success."
~ David Newman, author of Do It! Marketing

"Olivia has tapped into a new era of capitalism."
~ Mary Elizabeth Milbrand, Designer and Visionary at HeyMaryElizabeth

"Using facts and figures, cutting-edge research, time-tested social theories, and Olivia's impressive experience in the corporate sector as well as examples from her life journey, she convincingly illustrates that LOVE@WORK benefits everyone – from shareholders to executives to front line workers."
~ Rev. Laura M. George, J.D., Executive Director of The Oracle Institute and Oracle Institute Press, founder of the Valley of Light Community

"Corporate America would benefit greatly if LOVE@WORK were to become required reading for students in University Business programs."
~ Dr. Ruth Anderson, Founder, Enlightened World

"By updating who we are as leaders and how our organizations operate – by integrating love into the fabric, we transform our organizations and our experience of working in these organizations."
~ Maureen Metcalf I Metcalf & Associates, Inc. CEO/Founder Innovative Leadership Institute

"This book is a roadmap for transforming a business culture from fear-based to love-based, that ends in happier employees and customers and a bigger, more solid, bottom line."
~ Cynthia Stott, International Speaker Coach/Global Visibility Influencer

"You'll learn how to uncover your inspired purpose, powerful secrets to success, excellent tips for creating an inspired life plan, plus strategies for healing trauma and negative patterns."
~ Marlene Elizabeth, Certified Money Coach® and Bestselling Author of MONEYWINGS™

LOVE@WORK

The Essential Guide to a Life of Inspired Purpose

Marina,
To such a sweet glorious spirit! May your voice shine across the cosmos. And may your love touch the hearts of the masses. Much love,
Olivia

Olivia Parr-Rud, MS

Quantum Love Press

This book is a work of non-fiction.

For information contact; address www.oliviapr.com

ISBN: 978-1-7324352-0-9

First Edition: October 2018

Dedication

To Addison, Aiden, and all the young souls who are coming to lead us into a more loving future.

Acknowledgements

This book has been incubating for many years, I've had a few amazing coaches along the way. Thank you, Stevie Ray McHugh, for helping to steer my thinking and for your creative genius. You were instrumental in helping me flesh out the LOVE@WORK Method. Thank you, Michelle Depres, for your wisdom, guidance, and encouragement. It was in your guided visualization that the cover image emerged as well as many ideas for the content of my book. Thank you, Michelle Williams, for helping me find my voice and your masterful editing. Thank you, John Castagnini, for your guidance and encouragement to create the LOVE@WORK method and think about how to take it into the world. Thank you, David Pyle, for your generous help with headshots and photography. Your talent and professionalism are world class. Finally, thank you Rebecca Hall Gruyter for so many things. First you helped me groom my content and encouraged me to trust my voice. From there, you and your team handled the editing, formatting, and marketing for the launch. Thank you all for helping me bring this book to life.

I'd also like to thank my family. First thanks to my sister, Marjie Gargiulo, for your ace editing skills and encouragement. Thanks to sister, Beth White, and sister-in-law, Jill Parr, for your encouragement as well. And thank you to my kids, Brandon, Adam, and Vanessa Rud, and my daughter-in-law, Allison Rud – you continue to inspire me to be my best.

And finally, I'd like to thank my spiritual tribe who helped me in so many ways. First and foremost, thank you to Joe Diamo. Your generous spirit, unconditional love, and tireless encouragement and guidance towards a deeper spiritual connection were instrumental in helping me to bring this book forward. Thank you, Marilyn Reis for your thoughtful feedback and amazing editing prowess. And thank you to my tribe of friends and healers, Mary Hostetter, Glennis Walter Smith, Priya Beate, Adelyn Jones, Lora Terres, Logan Kline, Dylan Clements, and Antanas Vainius. You all kept me aligned, feeling good, laughing, and feeling loved and valued. You are all in my hearts forever.

An Invitation

Does your current job leave you feeling uninspired? Do you ever wish you felt more enthusiastic about your work?

Do you ever feel the need to hide who you really are? Would you love to express more of your authentic self? Do you have the desire to connect more deeply to others?

Do you yearn for more meaning in your work? Are you inspired to make a positive difference in the world? There is a reason for this…

Many of us are waking up… We yearn to make a difference – to use our innate gifts in a way that improves our lives and the lives of others. We want to be seen for *who* we are, not what we do. We yearn to connect, to be heard, to hear others. We ache to share our stories, our talents, and our passions – to make a positive difference in the world.

If this resonates with you, then I have good news! Not only are we waking up – Corporate America needs us to wake up! The businesses that are most successful today and will thrive going forward, are the ones that require us to show up fully and in deep connection with our hearts and the hearts of others.

Many years ago, I felt that yearning… I felt that disconnect from who I was and what I was doing.

After twenty years as a mom and fledging entrepreneur, I took a corporate job to support my family. The work culture was so hostile that I thought I had landed on another planet. As a lifelong spiritual seeker, I could not get my bearings. Working in an environment that was totally driven by fear was overwhelming.

Over the next ten years, I felt like I lived in two worlds. My business career blossomed. I wrote a book on data science that launched me onto the global stage. I began to get invitations to speak and consult. But the part of me that yearned for wholeness and a desire to share my true gifts felt unsafe. So, I kept that part of me hidden.

Then I read "The World is Flat" by Thomas Freeman. And I had an amazing insight! Simply put, I saw the connection between the growth of technology and the need for corporations to create a culture that invites us to feel seen, heard, and inspired by our work… a culture that benefits from each of us to have an open heart... a culture based on love.

For our businesses to thrive in today's fast-paced, high-tech, global economy, we must all be more agile and resilient. We must create a corporate culture that can adapt quickly to global market changes and pressures. This is possible only if we are encouraged to share our gifts, deeply trust each other, and work for the greater good.

We must all think of ourselves as leaders and value our human capital as our greatest asset. We must develop and nurture a culture based on caring, compassion, and connection, i.e. "Love."

The benefits of "Love" go way beyond Corporate America's bottom line. A culture of "Love" will heal our families, our communities, and the planet at large.

I invite you to take a journey with me – a journey of exploring, learning, healing, unveiling, releasing, discovering, intending, planning, daring, andthriving. Our planet has many challenges. Our very survival depends on each of us waking up, owning our power, sharing our gifts, and working together toward a more loving world.

Table of Contents

Foreword
Julie Roberts, PhD

As we enter into a time of increasing uncertainly and global volatility, I am heartened and encouraged by Olivia Parr-Rud's new book, ***LOVE@WORK***. Her approach not only offers hope and a positive outlook for our current situation. She offers a path for all of us to step into our power and be the leaders who can create a positive future.

I have come to believe that the most helpful thingwe can to do in this stage of our civilization is to go to our hearts and do our own work. This is what ***LOVE@WORK*** is all about. Olivia provides significant data to support her claim that love benefits the bottom line in the workplace. She also discusses the need to create loving organizations to help evolve our civilization and she provides steps to take to get there.

Though I now work almost exclusively with a methodology called CLEAR® that I developed to help people shift negative beliefs and patterns, I trained leaders and worked in organizations for over 30 years. In my organizational work I found that a healthy culture is dependent upon leaders *living* the values of the organization. This means that they are self-reflective and willing to hear feedback regarding their impact – which means they need be open to how they impact employees regarding their *own* behavior. Olivia assumes this in her book and her methods are self-reflective. How can we create loving organizations if we don't look first to ourselves?

Olivia also discusses the importance of employee engagement in the success of organizations. Organizations that have engaged employees are ones that create psychological safety so people feel safe to show up and share their thoughts and feelings. In order to create a culture of safety, leaders need to lead and behave in caring ways. In order to create loving organizations, we have to *be* the change we want to see, and so the first step (as Olivia says) is to love ourselves. Leaders need to instill loving behaviors in themselves before they can create an environment of love and safety in an organization.

When we are aligned with our purpose and values, we live a life that is more connected and loving to ourselves and thus to others. We honor our feelings and our drives and are thus more authentic, happier and more at peace. We are more in a flow with life. Once we are aligned with our own purpose, we are able to then align with an organization's purpose and values. Olivia guides us through a process to get in touch with that purpose and she then discusses bringing that purpose to the world. From that place of wholeness, we are all able to contribute to a loving culture in our work and our communities at large.

PART I
The Certainty of Love

What is Love? And why am I so certain it is essential for our success?

Let's start with "What is Love?"
Such a deep question.... Haven't poets and philosophers debated this for centuries?

Perhaps... But they are writing about romantic love. We're exploring the benefits of bringing love into business. This is new territory. We need precision! Let's start with Wikipedia.

"Love is a variety of different feelings, states, and attitudes that ranges from interpersonal affection ("I love my mother") to pleasure ("I loved that meal"). It can refer to an emotion of a strong attraction and personal attachment. It can also be avirtue representing human kindness, compassion, and affection—"the unselfish loyal and benevolent concern for the good of another." It may also describe compassionate and affectionate actions towards other humans, one's self or animals. (Wikipedia)"

"Why go to Wikipedia to define love?" For most of us, Wikipedia is the first place we go for factual, even if we don't always agree with what we find. Why?

Perhaps we know it considers the broadest, most diverse, and most current range of inputs. Changes can post quickly, and anyone from around the globe can refute its claims. In quantum terms, Wikipedia is a great example of emergent order – order that emerges from chaos. This is a powerful metaphor for agile corporations that thrive on a culture of love.

So, I'll use Wikipedia's last two definitions of love as a foundation for the meaning of Love in this book. In my mind, these clearly sum up what I mean when I talk about ***LOVE@WORK***.

> "[Love] can … be a virtue representing human kindness, compassion, and affection—'the unselfish loyal and benevolent concern for the good of another.' It may also describe compassionate and affectionate actions towards other humans, one's self or animals."

Let's explore why it's a good idea to bring love into business and the steps we can take to make that happen.

Chapter 1
Love of Money

If you resonated with my invitation then chances are you aspire to more than just getting rich. However, our economy only seems to work for those whohave money. So, I want to emphasize that by striving for a more loving business culture you are not choosing *"love"* over profits. In fact, the data suggests the exact opposite. Bringing loving concepts and practices into your business is very good for profits as well!

"If we're going to create thriving, innovative, respectful, collaborative, engaged cultures, that will produce solutions to our world's biggest challenges, 'love' needs to be expressed in our professional engagements."
- Margaret Hasna Kelsey, Ed.M.

In this chapter, we'll learn about real companies who are proving that "loving behavior" leads to the highest benefit for business while also having a positive effect on individuals, communities, and the planet at large.

Profiting with Love

Employee engagement is a huge driver of business success. A 2013 Gallup survey revealed that only 29 of US and Canada employees are engaged in their jobs. Western Europe has a 14% engagement rate with East Asia trailing at 6%. But this level of engagement can be improved through connection, compassion, and caring, i.e. 'love.'

In 2001, Campbell Soup's sales were plummeting. Rumors of a hostile takeover were brewing. 'The company had devolved into what one magazine called "a beleaguered old brand".' Something had to be done. Douglas Conant, the newly hired CEO, decided to tackle several areas, not the least of which was poor employee engagement. Based on a 2002 Gallup survey, 74% were either not actively engaged or actively disengaged – the worst ever polled in a Fortune 500 firm, according to Conant. Eight years later, the number of actively engaged employees rose to 63% with only 3% actively disengaged. How did Conant do it?

He immediately made some cosmetic changes to the property. Then he instructed his managers (many of whom were replaced) to meet with all their direct reports on a daily to update them on the company's progress. Conant also set an example – he sent our 20 thank-you notes a day to staffers at all levels. And he had regular lunch dates with small groups of employees to get their perspectives and invite feedback. **In other words, he demonstrated that he valued them and cared about what they thought connection and compassion.**

How did this lead to business success? Over the eight years following his cultural imperative, earnings per share grew 5% to 10% per year – putting Campbell's Soup at the top of its industry. Stocks (with reinvested dividends) returned over 30% in value over the same period while the Standard & Poor's 500 index lost more than 10%. Additional benefits, according to Conant, include a more innovative and self-governing workforce – additional benefits of a workforce that feels seen and valued, i.e. 'loved.'

Benefits of Love

You don't have to look far to see more financial benefits of love in business. SAS Institute, a large privately-owned software company with over $3 billion dollars in annual revenue, is a perfect example. They offer 7-hour work days, unlimited sick days (which can be used to care for sick family members), as well as onsite exercise, daycare, medical, and counseling facilities. The cafeteria has child seats and live music every day!

"Because we eliminate unnecessary distractions and help relieve everyday stress, our employees are happier, healthier and proud of the difference their work makes." – Jim Goodnight, CEO, SAS

And how do they benefit? SAS has enjoyed over two decades of double-digit growth. And their employee turnover rate is just 4%. Compare that to the industry average of 20% and the savings add up quickly.

In their groundbreaking book, *Leveraging the New Human Capital*, Sandra Barud and Marie Tumolo highlighted the high ROI realized by companies that offer child care, flexible work hours, and paid family leave.

- Childcare: Chase Manhattan's investment in backup childcare services for their employees resulted in a 115% ROI.
- Home Office: American Express introduced telecommuting which boosted sales by $40 million. Aetna saw a 30% increase in claims processing.
- Parental Leave: A 2001 study showed an increase in profits of 2.5% for companies offering parental leave.
- Benefits for Working Mothers: Companies on the "100 Best Companies for Working Mothers" offer child care benefits, flex scheduling, telecommuting, and more. They saw higher customer satisfaction ratings which translated into a 3% to 11% increase inmarket value.

Loving your employees by providing opportunities for wellness and fitness programs has also proven to boost profits.

- Pepsi's fitness program returned $3.00 for every $1.00 invested, an enviable 300% ROI.
- Johnson and Johnson introduced their Corporate Wellness Program and realized a net savings of roughly $225 per employee each year through fewer hospitalizations, mental health visits, and outpatient services.
- Steelcase saw a drop of 55% in medical claims over six years for participants in their wellness programs.

All the above examples are strong arguments for institutionalizing 'loving' behavior. Let's look at some more examples where the employee satisfaction was a distinguishing factor.

Love is the New Workplace Currency

"Every soul speaks the same language. Know that language of love that swells within the human temple." – Maharaj Ji

I don't know about you but I am amazed and thrilled that Love is even being named as a 'Currency' in business. Louis Carter, author of Change Champion's Field Guide and Best Practices in Talent Management books published by John Wiley & Sons, did extensive research into what drives employees to be loyal and hard-working. He found that the #1 reason why people produce more for their companies is loving their workplace.

Carter and his team surveyed over 175 companies across the US, Middle East/Northern Africa, Europe, and South East Asia. They analyzed what love of company means to them to create a model for a "Most Loved Workplace."

The "results were conclusive across geographies, organization size, and industries. People who loved their workplaces were 94% more likely to perform better and provide results, with 59% saying they are four times more likely."

They found that 94% of respondents were 2-4 times more likely to produce more for their organization if they love their workplace. And 95% of the respondents were 2-4 times more likely to stay at the company if they loved their workplace.

Analysis of the data clearly shows that getting respect drives a most loved workplace. "The result is to better performance, team cohesiveness, and reduced turnover. While some companies focus on compensation, promises of friendship, benefits, and perks to "buy" employee loyalty, this study finds that **a culture of respect for employees is the great equalizer. Respect is the new currency and one in which any business can supply in unlimited amounts if it so chooses.**"

"A feeling of love for the workplace far outweighed other measurements of employee outcomes such as commitment. It is loving one's workplace that showed the greatest validity in predicting workforce outcomes."

Stock Up on Love

You can even look at stock market returns to see the value of loving your employees. A study by Russell Investments compared the general stock returns for two groups of companies ranked in *CNN Money/Fortune Best 100 Companies to Work For* annual list. Their performance was compared to the Russell 3000 and the Standard & Poor's (S&P) 500 indexes between the years 1998 and 2014. The two "Best 100" groups were as follows:

- Portfolio A: At the beginning of 1998, equal amounts are invested in the stock of each of the "Best 100" publicly traded companies. At the end of each year, the portfolio was liquidated and invested in the newly selected "Best 100" publicly traded companies for the next year. This purchase and liquidation process were repeated each year up through 2014.
- Portfolio B: At the beginning of 1998, equal amounts are invested in the stock of each of the "Best 100" publicly traded companies. The stock was held with the same companies through the end of 2014.

The results were remarkable. The annualized return for the "100 Best" companies in Portfolio A (11.07%) and Portfolio B (12.71%) were around twice the annualized returns for the Russell 3000 (6.76%) and the S&P 500 (6.48%). The cumulative return was roughly 200% higher for Portfolio A (548.0%) and Portfolio B (664.2%) compared to Russell 3000 (204.0%) and the S&P 500 (190.7%).

Love of Engagement

Employee engagement is defined as "a property of the relationship between an organization and its employees. An "engaged employee" is defined as one who is fully absorbed by and enthusiastic about their work and so takes positive action to further the organization's reputation and interests." According to the Society of Human Resources Management Report sponsored by Randstad, companies with highly engaged employees enjoy savings in a number of ways.

- At Molson Coors, strong employee engagement saved the company over $1.7 million in safety costs over a year. Highly engaged employees were much less likely to have a safety incident than non-engaged employees.

- Caterpillar increased employee engagement and saw less attrition, absenteeism and overtime at one European plant which resulted in a savings of $8.8 million annually as well as a $2 million increase in profits and a 34% increase in customer satisfaction.

While the above results are remarkable, the companies were selected solely based on the levels of employee engagement and satisfaction. They don't consider any other stakeholders. In the following section, I'll show how companies that show 'love' for all stakeholders are formula for even higher profits.

Firms of Endearment

In one of my favorite books on how I think of love in business, *Firms of Endearment*, Raj Sisodia, David Wolfe, and Jag Sheth point out how "the words affection, love, joy, authenticity, empathy, compassion, soulfulness, and other terms of endearment" have historically had no place in business. However, they are becoming more common today.

The authors coined the phrase "Firms of Endearment," or FoE, to represent companies that endear themselves to the stakeholders by bringing the interests of all stakeholders into strategic alignment. This includes employees, suppliers, the communities in which they operate, as well as the stockholders. Capitalism is often considered an economic concept without a soul. Its only purpose is to benefit shareholders. However, advances in technology and globalization are stressing this short-sighted model and transforming capitalism. The authors put it this way. "The nature of the transformation can be summed up in one short statement: Companies are increasingly motivated by and being held accountable for humanistic as well as economic performance."

This is indeed good news because a majority of today's young workers and many of the rest ofus are hungry for an economy that cares as much for humans as it does for profits. In fact, we want an economic system that cares for the planet as well.

Many companies focus on "share of wallet." Companies that qualified as Firms of Endearment (FoEs) are more interested in "share of heart." The logic is that if you earn a place in your customer's heart, you will get a bigger share of your customer's wallet. This goes for employees, suppliers, and communities in which these companies operate. I'll expand on the philosophy of Firms of Endearment in Chapter 4

To qualify as a Firm of Endearment, the researchers asked people what companies they loved, and why. They asked if the world is a better place because this company exists. And they asked if the customers and employees are loyal along with a number of other questions.

Quantifiable benefits were realized as a result of capturing "share of heart." After narrowing the list to 28 public and private companies who best manifested a high standard of humanistic performance, the researchers performed an analysis from an investor viewpoint. **They found that the public FoEs returned 1,026% t for investors over the ten years ending June 30, 2006, compared to 122% for the S&P 500; that's more than an 8-to-1 ratio.**

They also compared their publicly traded companies to the 11 *Good to Great* companies detailed in Jim Collins' best-selling book *Good to Great.* Just as a reminder, the companies identified as "great" in *Good to Great* are ones that performs well for investors. None qualified as a Firm of Endearment which must "spread joy and fulfillment and make the world a better place because it exists." The results showed:

- Over a 10-year period, the 13 public FoEs outperformed the *Good to Great* companies 1,026% to 331% (a 3-to-1 ratio).
- Over a 5-year period, 17 FoEs outperformed the *Good to Great* companies 128% to 77% (1 1.7-to-1 ratio).

- Over a 3-year period, 18 FoEs performed statistically on par with the *Good to Great* companies: 73% to 75%.

In the second addition of Firms of Endearment, the authors wanted to broaden the range of companies to include additional industries. They also wanted to apply greater rigor to the selection process. They scored companies based on a few criteria: 1) a nuanced balance of "a well-articulated and authentically lived purpose that goes beyond profit maximization;" 2) a "purpose driven, service-minded, and reasonably paid CEO;" 3) "evidence that the companies had cultures that were rooted in trust, caring, and authenticity." Companies whose cultures were fear-based and highly competitive were rejected. The difference in financial performance is nothing short of spectacular:

- Over a 3-year period, the cumulative returns for the US FoEs were 83.37% compared to the S&P 500 at 57.00%. In this short time window, Good to Great companies outperformed the FoEs with a return rate of 221.81%. In my opinion, this is due to their cultural characteristics which favor short term gain.

- Over a 5-year period, the cumulative returns for the US FoEs were 151.34% which is slightly lower than the Good to Great companies at 158.45% but over twice that of the S&P 500 at 60.87%.

- Over a 10-year period, the cumulative returns for the US FoEs was 409.66% compared to the Good to Great companies at 175.80% and the S&P 500 at 107.03%.

- Over a 15-year period, the cumulative returns for the US FoEs was 1681.11% compared to the Good to Great companies at 262.91% and the S&P 500 at 117.64%.

These results are nothing short of remarkable! I'm not aware of any other strategy or tactic produces returns like these. It must be the 'love' factor!

Love that Brand

Love is also taking over marketing! Kevin Roberts is CEO of one of the world's largest ad agencies, Saatchi & Saatchi. In his book, *Lovemarks: The Future Beyond Brands*, he claims that love should be the foundation of all marketing:

At Saatchi & Saatchi, our pursuit of Love and what it could mean for business has been focused and intense. Human beings need Love. Without it they die. Love is about responding, about delicate, intuitive sensing. Love is always two-way. When it is not, it cannot live up to the name Love.
Love cannot be commanded or demanded. It can only be given.

Former Yahoo! Chief Solutions Officer, Tim Sanders, strongly supports love as the solution. In his book, *Love Is the Killer App: how to Win Business and Influence Friends*, he expresses beautifully:

I don't think there is anything higher than Love…. Love is so expansive. I had such a difficult time coming up with a definition for Love in my book, but the way I define Love is the selfless promotion of the growth of the other.

Zappos

Zappos is famous for their customer service. Early on, the leadership team decided to make their customers feel loved. They might not have explicitly stated it that way. But they certainly create a loving atmosphere.

Zappos Family Core Values

One of the strengths of Zappos is their commitment to a set of core values. Since they think of their employees as family, they declare their core family values Zappos is committed to evolving their values as they develop their culture, their brand, and their business strategies. These are the ten core values that they live by:

1. Deliver WOW Through Service
2. Embrace and Drive Change
3. Create Fun and A Little Weirdness
4. Be Adventurous, Creative, and Open-Minded
5. Pursue Growth and Learning

6. Build Open and Honest Relationships with Communication
7. Build a Positive Team and Family Spirit
8. Do More with Less
9. Be Passionate and Determined
10. Be Humble

These ten values create what I would consider a very loving environment.

Vail Resorts

"Love at Vail Resorts means creating incredible experiences for guests and our employees. Vail Resorts recognizes that cultivating the passion, connection and joy of employees has a direct effect on customer joy and happiness. - Jeff Klem, VP, Talent Management. Vail Resorts, Boulder, Colorado."

Southwest Airlines

"A company is stronger if it is bound by love rather than by fear."
– Herb Kelleher, CEO

Every business book ever written drives home the point that the culture starts at the top. This is nowhere more apparent than with Southwest Airlines. And the employees walk the talk. They have a true culture of love and it's paying off.

Mission

"The **mission** of **Southwest Airlines** is dedication to the highest quality of Customer Service delivered with a sense of warmth, friendliness, individual pride, and Company Spirit. We are committed to provide our Employees a stable work environment with equal opportunity for learning and personal growth."

Purpose

"Connect People to what's important in their lives through friendly, reliable, and low-cost air travel."

Vision

"To become the world's most loved, most flown, and most profitable airline."

Values

The employees are encouraged "Live the Southwest Way" which invites a Warrior Spirit, a Servant's Heart, and a Fun-LUVing Attitude.

The employees are encouraged "Work the Southwest Way" which includes Safety and Reliability, Friendly Customer Service, and Low Costs.

Subaru

Subaru literally makes a love promise! They state their intention in very loving terms.

The Subaru Love Promise

"Subaru and its retailers believe in making the world a better place and the Subaru Love Promise is our vision of respecting all people. This is our promise to show love and respect to our customers and to work to make a positive impact in the world."

As we look deeper into the Subaru philosophy, we see that loving behavior is at the heart of this company.

"At Subaru of America we are committed to the vitality of our people, to the health of our planet, and to enhancing the communities where we live and work. Our corporate responsibility efforts and philanthropic commitments address the issues our employees, customers and communities are passionate about and we strive to address these issues in ways that allow us to create positive change – within our operations and beyond our four walls."

Final Thoughts

I find it inspiring that so many companies have implemented 'loving' practices and realized the financial benefits as a result. Can you imagine what it would be like to have some of these loving characteristics in your place of work?

While higher profits should be reason enough to bring love in your business, in the next chapter, I share powerful evolutionary trends that support the concept that our consciousness is evolving – a trend that supports the importance of love as a key driver of business success.

Reflections

Think about the companies that give you a good feeling. Search for their mission statement online. Read articles about and by members of their management team. See if their mission statement aligns with a company that embraces love as a way of doing business. Remember, they don't necessarily have to use the word 'love.' Look for leaders and mission statements that values people, culture, and sustainability for the planet.

Chapter 2
Our Evolving Consciousness

"The rapid spread of an evolved consciousness is crucial for humanity's future. Whether such consciousness reaches a critical mass will decide if humanity moves in "time from the 'business as usual' scenario leading to breakdown to the transformation scenario that leads toward a new civilization." – Ervin Laszlo

If you are young or you've had a lot of exciting life experiences, you may be someone who gets bored unless you have new challenges coming at you all the time. On the other hand, if you are someone who likes your life to be very predictable, then you may wish you could go back to the good old days. In my long corporate career, I've experienced both. Early in my career, rapid change and new technologies intimidated me. As time passed, I grew accustomed to the constant change. Now I get bored if I'm not taking on new challenges.

I feel there is a reason for this accelerated change. Technology is driving us towards greater complexity. This trend forces us to take a more holistic view that encompasses a myriad of interrelated parts. Given this challenge, we are starting to realize that we are better able to solve complex problems if we do two things:

1) tap our innate wisdom; and
2) tap the wisdom of our tribes. Before we get into the 'how,' let's look at the 'why.'

"It is not the strongest of the species that survive, nor is it the most intelligent, but the one most responsive to change." – Charles Darwin

In this chapter, we'll look at several models that map the evolution of humanity as it adapts to increasing complexity.

As I mentioned, one of the biggest drivers of complexity is rapidly evolving technological landscape. In Kevin Kelly's latest book, *"What Technology Wants,"* Kevin offers a thought-provoking list of what the cosmos, life, and technology are all selecting for:

- Increasing efficiency
- Increasing opportunity
- Increasing emergence
- Increasing complexity
- Increasing diversity
- Increasing specialization
- Increasing ubiquity
- Increasing freedom
- Increasing mutualism
- Increasing beauty
- Increasing sentience
- Increasing structure
- Increasing evolvability

This list of trends allows us to consider whether new technology serve the few or the whole. We may want to evaluate them on how they increase or decrease "diversity, sentience, opportunity, mutuality, ubiquity, etc.

In my own career, I have seen a tremendous acceleration of technology. When I first started developing statistical models in 1991, I had a computer with a 500 MB hard drive. The processing time for one logistic regression model was 27 hours. Today, the processing time for the same logistic regression model is less than 10 seconds! And there is a myriad of additional options powered by the exponential increase in computing power.

As we look at our evolving consciousness as individuals, society, and companies; let's look at what current theories and research can enrich our understanding.

Stages of Consciousness

Many great theorists have developed models to help us understand and navigate our increasingly complex world. These models provide a roadmap through which to view our evolution of consciousness over thousands of years. The underlying theories of our characteristics and behaviors suggest a trajectory that offers hope for our future.

"…the most difficult, but at the same time the most exciting transition the human race has faced to date. It is not merely a transition to a new level of existence but the start of a new "movement" in the symphony of human history." – Dr. Clare W. Graves

Early research of the evolution of consciousness was pioneered by Dr. Graves and resulted in his theory of Spiral Dynamics. Dr. Graves felt that in response to the ever-changing conditions, we as individuals and societies evolved through stages by way of a spiral process. He believed that the more complexity we experienced, the more complex our behavior displayed. Each stage, with its distinct problems and solutions, allows us to make meaning within our distinct world view.

"Each successive stage, wave, or level of existence is a state through which people pass on their way to other states of being. When the human is centralized in one state of existence, he or she has a psychology which is particular to that state. His or her feelings, motivations, ethics and values, biochemistry degree of neurological activation, learning systems, belief systems, education, economic, and political theory and practice are all appropriate to that state."

According to Dr. Graves, the development of consciousness is an open-ended process with eight stages identified so far. His research was expanded to nine stages by Ken Wilbur, considered one of the greatest living philosophers, and Dr. Laura George, founder and director of the Oracle Institute. The following is a brief description of each stage:

1. Survival/Archaic
2. Tribal
3. Egocentric
4. Authoritarian/Traditional

5. Enterprising/Modernist
6. Humanistic/Post Modern
7. Integrative/Emergent Integral
8. New-Tribal/Mature Integral
9. Transcendental

To gain a deeper understanding, refer to the expanded descriptions of the nine stages in the Appendix.

As we track our human competencies through these nine stages, one significant characteristic is that each stage shows increased complexity and sophistication. This trend may be preparing us to better manage the increasing complexity being introduced by advances in technology and increasing global connectivity.

Barrett's Seven Levels of Consciousness

A practical model that I feel is especially useful in business is "The Seven Levels of Consciousness" by Richard Barrett – based on Maslow's hierarchy of needs, these seven levels offer a map of the evolution for our organizations. In "Happier at Work", Gayle Van Gils expands on Barrett's work by offering seven levels as they relate to our personal lives. The following is a brief description of each level:

1. Survival
2. Relationship
3. Performance
4. Improvement
5. Alignment
6. Collaboration
7. Service

For a full description of all seven levels, please refer to the Appendix.

Tracking to the Stages of Consciousness suggested by Graves, Wilbur, and George, Barrett's Seven Levels reveal how our personalities evolve through the levels. By observing our behaviors and aspirations through Barrett's Seven Levels, we can get a sense of where we are and what behaviors we might want to adopt to reach the next level. Similarly, in our organizational, we can evaluate at what level our teams or departments are and what we need to do to evolve to the next level within our organizations.

Theory of Social Maturity

Another model that I find helpful for understanding our evolution is Robert Kegan's Theory of Social Maturity. Social Maturity becomes increasingly valuable as our world grows more complex. As uncertainty becomes more common, we feel more stress in our home and work lives. Advancing our Social Maturity equips us to better manage our stress.

To understand Kegan's theory, we must understand subject-object consciousness. Subject consciousness refers to those self-concepts to which we are so attached that we cannot take an objective viewpoint. This can be problematic when we face difficult situations.

Object consciousness, on the other hand, is a self- concept that we are now able to view a situation objectively. Therefore, in each stage, what was subject consciousness in the prior stage evolves to object consciousness, i.e. a concept that we can view objectively.

This can be seen in babies who have no sense of the other. Everything is an extension of self. As they mature, they begin to differentiate themselves from other people and objects in their environment.

Kegan suggests that we pass through discrete stages of social maturity. When we move into a new stage, we are in a dynamic process of evolving our subject consciousness into object consciousness. The more we mature, the better we become at moving beyond our own perspective and gain the ability to think abstractly and imagine another person's perspective. This is the basis of compassion. For a complete description of the Levels of Social Maturity, please refer to the Appendix.

Evolution through Generations

When I landed my first big corporate job, I was 40 years young. Everyone else on my team, except my manager, was in their mid to late 20s. Oddly, I never felt older probably because I don't think like most people in my age group. In generational terms, I'm known as a 'baby boomer.'

The terms 'Baby Boomer', Gen X, Gen Y, and Millennials are thrown around quite a bit these days to explain different attitudes and trends. But the truth is, the cultures are different – partly because their experiences growing up were different. And I would also argue that each subsequent generation displays a higher level of consciousness.

Before you look for exceptions, I am just making the point that there are general trends in the culture. And people of each generation tend to settle down to live near other people with whom they share cultural and spiritual values.

Let's look at each generation, the approximate range of years, and what events and trends shaped their culture. As you read about each generation, think about how this affects all of us connecting and working towards a common goal. Also, think about the power of bringing multiple generations together.... leveraging all the respective strengths.

The G.I. Generation

Coined the Greatest Generation by Tom Brokaw, the G.I. Generation roughly ranges from 1901 to 1924-27. This generation was dominated by World War II which ignited a cultural shift. Prior to WWII, men held positions of power in the home and in the workplace. Women were scarce in the workplace. As WWII took many men overseas, the women took charge in the home.

Due to shortages in the factories, many women started working outside the home. "Rosie the Riveter" became famous as a symbol for women by showing her strength and power in the building trades.

To get a sense of their level of consciousness, think of someone you know who was born before 1946. Do you think they are the kind of person who loves change and quickly adapts to new technologies? Probably not! My sister, who is right on the boundary of that age group, retired recently from a long career that required her to use the latest technologies. Now, she coaches senior citizens on how to use email and social media. She says that many of from the G.I. Generation have fears of using technology.

I also feel that people of this generation were better at suppressing their emotions. They compartmentalized their war experiences and never processed their feelings about the horrors they experienced. This speaks to how our brains are evolving. Subsequent generations are less able to live emotionally healthy lives following their military experience. They have more psychological issues such as PTSD.

The Silent Generation

Often called "The Lucky Few", members of this generation were generally born from 1925 to 1944. Their adult lives spanned WWII, Korea, and the beginning of the Vietnam war. They initiated a surge in the divorce rate and popularized the term "midlife crisis." The timing of their rise to adulthood gave them the economic advantage of the post WWII booming economy already in progress. As a result, they have enjoyed financial security throughout their lives.

Baby Boomers

Following WWII, many veterans returned to a burgeoning economy and started families. Spanning approximately 1943 to 1960, the Baby Boomer generation represents 65 million adults today. Unlike the generation before us, many of us were raised on processed food and early television. As young adults, we enjoyed the freedom of "the pill" and endured the horrors of the Vietnam War. According to U.S. Trust, Boomers are the first generation to feel that giving their kids good values is more important than providing them with wealth. This may represent a trend towards higher consciousness.

Generation X

Gen X'ers were born primarily between 1964 and 1981. A smaller generation, many grew up in families with two working parents. So, they were often invisible and took care of themselves. As they aged, they shied away from the mainstream career and religious institutions. Instead they found their place outside of big institutions and organized religion. As the most highly educated generation, they are quietly making huge changes by taking on managementroles and mentoring their coworkers. Hailing innovators like Elon Musk, they are currently 55% of startup founders. They are very much at ease with technology and often live in intergenerational homes. They easily navigate the digital world with 80% on Facebook.

Xennials

The Xennials are a micro generation that were born between 1977 and 1983 – the cusp years of the Gen Xers and the Millennials. They are the only generation to reach adulthood as we transitioned from analogue to digital. Many possess both Gen X cynicism and Millennial optimism and drive.

Australian Dan Woodman, associate professor of Sociology at the University of Melbourne, claims that Xennials have a more unique perspective on technology.

'The idea is there's this micro or in-between generation between the Gen X group – who we think of as the depressed flannelette-shirt-wearing, grunge- listening children that came after the Baby Boomers and the Millennials – who get described asoptimistic, tech savvy and maybe a little bit too sure of themselves and too confident,' Professor Woodman told the Daily Mail.

Xennials grew up with landline and kept up with current events through radio and television. Then in their early 20s, the tech boom hit and they became very tech-savvy.

Millennials

Born in the 80s and 90s, Millennials, or Gen Y'ers, are the most ethnically and racially diverse generation ever. Considered by some to be narcissistic, they are driven by self-expression. They are highly adept at leveraging technology to share everything from their dinner to their dream vacation.

In an article on Forbes.com "What Millennials Want In The Workplace (And Why You Should Start Giving It To Them)", Rob Asghar cites a study by the Intelligence Group that reveals the level of consciousness of Millennial workers:

1. 64% of them say it's a priority for them to make the world a better place.
2. 72% would like to be their own boss. But if they do have to work for a boss, 79% of them would want that boss to serve more as a coach or mentor.
3. 88% prefer a collaborative work-culture rather than a competitive one.
4. 74% want flexible work schedules.
5. And 88% want "work-life integration," which isn't the same as work-life balance, since work and life now blend together inextricably.

So, if you resonate with these values, take heart! You are steadily gaining control.

Generation Z

Born between the mid 1990's and early 2000's, their workplace values are just beginning to form. As the children of Gen X'ers. They are the first "truly global generation." They are highly connected with their peers which diminishes the influence of their parents. Their career decisions are more motivated by curiosity, money, and the opportunity to help others. Having grown up in a post 9/11 world, they are more realistic and pragmatic than the Gen Y'ers.

"A recent Gen Z-focused issue of The Cassandra Report, states that "43% of 7 to 13-year-olds feel that school violence/shootings will have the biggest impact on their generation, overriding the invention of social networking and the election of the first Black President.

They may be experiencing an early loss of innocence, but their upbringing has made them resilient and pragmatic. Rather than hide from their problems, they want to understand and confront them."

Think how powerful it could be for individuals, corporations and our society at large if we tapped into the respective strengths of each generation. I feel this is possible if we can encourage our corporate leaders to invite diversity and value multiple perspectives.

Our Evolving Brains

Have you ever thought about what you desire and how your desires change over time? When I was young, I was immersed in a culture that told me that material possessions would make me happy. Today, after years of personal growth and healing, I can't shed my material possessions fast enough. To relax, I long to be in nature – to get away from my 'stuff,' especially technology.

There is strong evidence that technology is evolving our brain. Several technologies have changed the way we used our brains. These changes in usage have caused different parts of our brain to become dominant while causing other parts of our brain to grow dormant. For our survival, I feel we need to use every part of our brain.

Let's look at a few early technologies that caused our brains to work differently. Prior to the invention of the map, humans used the positions of celestial objects and their intuition to navigate the globe. Maps introduced a whole new way of looking at the world. In addition to the practical uses of charting routes and establishing boundaries, maps trained us to think more abstractly.

Clocks are another invention that radically changed the way we used our brains. Can you even imagine your life without a clock? Prior to this invention, humans were in tune with the rhythms of nature.

They followed the natural flow of the seasons and celestial patterns. Today, our lives are dictated by precise, discrete, measurable units of time.

The printing press is considered one of the most significant inventions for the evolution of humanity. Previously available only to the wealthy and priestly classes, knowledge was suddenly available to the commoner who was inspired to master reading, writing, and arithmetic. With the newly acquired skills dominated by the left brain, society changed rapidly. It brought on a "feeling of autonomy, individuality, spirit of competition, discovery, innovation, control, and domination."

"The brain that ushered the Europeans into the world of territorial exploration, science, and technology in the eighteenth and nineteenth centuries was … the left brain – the aggressive and dominant part of our brain that thinks it knows everything." Think ego!

This domination by the left brain sowed the seeds of modernity and post modernity. Great thinkers set out to find solutions for age-old problems using the rational mind or left brain. Right brain thinking lost credibility. Intuition and sacred knowledge were marginalized or discredited.

Carl Sagan, the famous astrophysicist felt that humans have made significant contributions to civilization – religion, culture, art, music, architecture, science, legal systems, ethical norms, and technology – because of the optimal balancing of the left and right brain. But with modernity, the left brain gained and remains in control a majority of the time.

The invention of photography and movies marked a turning point back towards balancing the use of both sides of the brain. The right brain can handle non- linear patterns and complexity. It specializes in imaginary and creative styles of thinking. It's the source of our intuition. So, when viewing a picture, the right brain grasps the complexity and non-linear patters. Then the left brain helps the right brain interpret the patterns draw objective conclusions.

Today there are a myriad of inventions that utilize the whole brain.

And the challenges we face demandthat we engage both sides of our brain. According to Rebecca Costa, author of "The Watchman's Rattle", our intuition is far superior to our left brain for solving critical problems quickly. Intuition may be just what we need to tackle the enormous problems in the world today.

The Three Turnings

One of my favorite models for personal evolution provides a beautiful segue into the next section of our journey. In her inspiring book, "Spiraling Upward, 5 Co-creative Processes for Women on the Rise," Wendy Wallbridge defines her view of evolution that applies beautifully to everyone seeking a life of Inspired Purpose.

The Spiral, which is characterized by ThreeTurnings, offers us a map of understanding our experience as we stay open and receptive to what is emerging. The following is a quick summary of the three turning points. See if you identify with any.

Initiation: The First Turning

"We awaken from a life by default and enter the First Turning of the Spiral through what I call an initiation-often activated by a loss, heartbreak, illness, or melancholy, or simply by finding ourselves in unchartered waters. At this point we have to choose to be fully responsible, conscious co- creators and authors of our lives. In the First Turning of the Spiral we learn ways to shift our identification from thoughts and feelings that make us suffer to a deeper, more genuine part of us that longs to open our hearts and enlighten our minds."

Aspiration: The Second Turning

The word that describes our innermost essence, our spirit, derives from the Latin word spiritus, meaning "breath," "air." We enter the Second Turning of the Spiral when we realize that beyond our egoic selves is an almighty, universal energy that is being "breathed" through us. We can experience this as a fierce longing to bring higher levels of truth, beauty, and goodness to the world. Here, at this Second Turning, we shift from "What's in it for me?" to "How can I become the best, most authentic version of myself?"

Inspiration: The Third Turning

The word inspire is defined as "to fill with an animating, quickening, or exalting influence." Inspiration isn't something we need to talk ourselves into – it just lifts us up. It is the creative principle expressed when we feel the first of I gotta do it! It is a pregnant ideal or feeling that enthusiastically prompts us to express our gifts. It is what lights us up and brings shine to our eyes. It uses us to answer the question, "How can I serve?"

– Wendy Wallbridge, with permission from Spiraling Upward

I love The Three Turnings for their clarity and simplicity. In the next chapter, we will reflect on these 'Turnings' as a signpost for our own conscious evolution.

Final Thoughts

I feel that all these models and their correlation to technological trends and advances in consciousness offer a hopeful message – in many ways, we are evolving as a species. How we use technology plays a huge role. And how we connect, care, and love each other plays an even bigger role. **If we can evolve into more loving, connected, caring humans, we can grow our businesses and bring joy into every area of our lives.**

Reflections

I invite you to reflect on each of these models. See if any of them offer more understanding of where you might be in your own journey or that of your organization. Think about where you want to go and whom you want to become.

PART II
The LOVE@WORK Method™

If you made it this far, you probably answered 'Yes' to at least some of the questions posed in "My Invitation." This indicates that you have probably entered the "Spiral" as defined by Wendy Wallbridge in the last chapter.""

When I first read about these three Turnings described in Chapter 2, I could so clearly see my life mapped within them. My first turning was initiated by loss and fear.

I spent many years feeling deeply insecure and often paralyzed by fear. And yet there was something within me that kept nudging me to move forward. I felt asif there was some spark of inspiration in me that could not be extinguished, even in my darkest hours.

As I searched for answers, I discovered powerful techniques and tools that allowed me to heal and connect more deeply with my internal spark. Once I made the decision that I wanted to show up for myself and heal, each day got easier. Eventually, my inspiration grew into a 'knowing' that I had an inspired purpose – some might call it a soul purpose. When I felt into the idea of my soul purpose, I felt a surge of energy that fueled me to keep searching for answers from many sources – mostly deep within myself.

If you feel some spark of inspiration or a drive that compels you, if you want to make a difference but you aren't sure how to proceed – then you will benefit from the LOVE@WORK Method. *My hope is that you will discover who you are, embrace your magnificent self, discover your Superpowers, step into your Inspired Purpose, and share your gifts with the world from a place of deep inspiration and gratitude.*

This method gives you the strength to connect deeply with yourself, take risks, and live in alignment with you Inspired Purpose. I share it with you from a place of deep gratitude for every one of my personal experiences, both negative and positive. I invite you to join me on this amazing journey.

Overview of LOVE@WORK Method™

Over the years, I've distilled the LOVE@WORK Method™ into four steps. As you work through the steps, you are empowered to discover and align with your inspired purpose in your career and in your life. Along the way, you will discover your true self, unveil and release the barriers that get in your way, and learn to show up for yourself and others. The LOVE@WORK Method™ offers techniques and practices to allow you to heal, align with your inspired purpose, and share your gifts in the world every day.

Along the way, you will find that by deeply loving yourself and opening your heart, you will tap into your own innate wisdom. This connection to your deepest self will empower you to enjoy unbridled creativity, deeply meaningful relationships, and an abundance of joy at work and at play.

"I am he and you are he and you are me and we are all together."
– The Beatles

A foundational principle of the LOVE@WORK Method™ is that we live in an interconnected, co- creative universe. Therefore, our paths and destinies are integrally connected with everyone and everything on the planet. **Whatever we want to manifest, create, attract, and experience must be desired for the greater good. I believe that as we seek to live an inspired life, we increase the chance that everyone else on the planet will thrive.**

The four steps of the LOVE@WORK Method™ follow a logical sequence. However, it may not be a direct path. Think of it more like a spiral. You will consistently progress to a higher level. But as you move through steps two through four, issues may arise that gently (or not so gently) nudge you back to an earlier step for more self-love, self-ownership, or clarity of purpose. Any time you move ahead to a new step and feel stuck or blocked, the LOVE@WORK Method™ will guide you back to the appropriate step with a couple of simple questions. Know that if find yourself going back through each step, you are still progressing…

Here are the four steps of the ***LOVE@WORKMethod™...***

Step 1: Love All of Yourself

Many of us find it easy to love others but struggle to really love every part of ourselves. And yet ifwe seek to live an inspired life, we must practice deep self-love and compassion. As we strive to love ourselves, we may experience resistance caused by unconscious patterns, limiting beliefs, and past traumas. This step guides you through practices and techniques for getting to a place of deep self-love. NOTE: Often mistaken for narcissism, self-love is not self-absorption. Self-love is characterized by behaviors such as generosity, humility, and kindness.

Step 2: Own Your Superpower

Many of us yearn to step into our power and express our unique gifts. Once you catch a glimpse of your potential, there is no going back. You can no longer hide your light. **Discovering and owning your Superpower is the next step in creating the career of your dreams and the life you were meant to live.** This step offers tools and practices that serve to unveil your unique gifts and innate wisdom that the world needs you to share.

Step 3: Visualize Your Inspired Purpose

As we gain more insight into our inspired purpose, we can start to imagine, visualize, and gain clarity around who we want to become or how we want to participate in the world. This step guides you to visualize your inspired purpose based on your Superpower or Superpowers. You create an inspired plan that clarifies how you want to be in the world and builds action steps to move into the world with your inspired purpose.

Step 4: Engage with Your Tribe

Historically, those of us who sought to live an inspired life would spend our lives in a monastery or on a secluded mountain top. It takes a lot of courage and will power to survive in this world, let alone feel inspired. But as we know, **the world needs us to show up fully and share our gifts. We need to shine our light everywhere we go. This includes the workplace. This step offers strategies for finding ways to open your heart, allow yourself to be vulnerable, and enjoy deep connection with your coworkers.** You will learn techniques for finding your inner calm in stressful environments. And you learn strategies and tools for moving through your fear so you can share your authentic self and truly shine your light.

Chapter 3

Love All of Yourself

Step one in the LOVE@WORK Method™ is Love all of Yourself. Making the decision to bring more love and inspiration into your work and life is the first step on your magnificent healing journey.

As we each step onto our path, we must acknowledge that we are very complex beings. Our thoughts and actions are often motivated or sabotaged by unconscious beliefs or experiences from our childhood. Once we make the decision to show up for ourselves, we may feel resistance or experience blocks that are triggered by our unconscious beliefs or traumas. Clearing and moving beyond these blocks are the first steps in to deep healing.

The more we love ourselves, the better care we take of ourselves. As we heal, we may still get upset or feel stuck. But we are less reactive and unlikely to blame others. As we take extreme ownership for every aspect of our life, we make better choices and have fewer regrets. **To be our authentic self and express our inspired purpose in our work and life, we must learn to love every part of ourselves.**

In this chapter, I'll share some of my personal healing story. I'll offer insights about how our early experiences shape our ability to love ourselves. And together, we'll explore powerful techniques for deepening our connection with ourselves. While you may feel overwhelmed at times, I encourage you to trust the process. You will be rewarded handsomely as you discover the true 'You' – the "You" that the world needs you to be!

What is Self-Love?

I feel that self-love is foundational to living an inspired life. Self-love is the core energetic state from which our inspiration flows. This flow allows us to truly show up, share our innate gifts, and make a positive difference in the world.

What self-love is not… Have you ever heard someone say, "He loves himself a bit too much!" I'm sure you've experienced that person who always wants to be the center of attention. The sad truth is that person is the one who needs more self-love. The person with a healthy level of self-love is comfortable when attention is on them while often insuring that it is balanced by directing attention to or showing appreciation for others.

If you simply practice putting your attention on others, your life will improve. Everyone wants to be seen, heard, and valued. By giving someone that gift, you will often be reciprocated with appreciation and love. All of this seems so simple. But how do we become capable of this?

Know Thyself

"Knowing yourself is the beginning of all wisdom" - Aristotle

Self-knowledge is essential to our ability to love ourselves. Self-knowledge is primarily gained through self-observation and self-discovery. By observing our behaviors and exploring our experiences, we gain insights into our deepest fears as well as our greatest strengths. By going deep within and asking simple, yet powerful questions, we can recognize our wounds and discover our greatest Superpower.

I was in my mid-40s before I had any capacity for self- observation or self-inquiry. Before that, I functioned primarily in survival mode. I'm pretty sure I know why.

By the time I was 20, I had lost both parents. My father died when I was five years old in a plane crash. At nineteen, I barely survived a near-fatal car accident. At twenty, my mother died of cancer. I was lost and scared. I had no idea who I was or why I was here.

Still dealing with significant health issues from my car accident, the loss of my mother was the final emotional blow. I felt like the ground had been ripped out from under me. I remember thinking that it wasn't safe to feel love. So, to ensure I never experienced that level of emotional pain again, I made the decision to numb my feelings and live in my head. Lucky for me, my left brain functioned well enough to survive. Many years later, I learned that most of my choices were driven by my deeply unconscious wound of abandonment.

"There is a crack in everything. That's how the light gets in."
- Leonard Cohen

"Who is this blubbering idiot?" I asked myself as I sat sobbing in front of this stranger who was my new therapist. "I can't seem to stop crying" I kept saying…

Here I was, a middle-aged woman. I'd been married for over twenty years and had three kids. But something in me was breaking open. My years of deep personal and spiritual work were forcing cracks inmy hardened façade. As I shared my life story, my new therapist said something that hit me like a ton of bricks, "You whole life is a series of abandonments." "Wow" I thought… "He's right!"

I still have vivid memories of my mother collapsing on the floor in tears. I was five. My grandfather arrived at our house unexpectedly to share the tragic news. My father had died in a plane crash.

At the time, I was mostly confused. I had no idea what death meant. I remember telling my friends that my daddy had died. I didn't realize it meant that I would never see him again.

My siblings and I had no grief counseling. The belief was that we were too young to remember any of this. My little brother returned to many of his infant behaviors.

As our lives changed to adjust to our new reality, I experienced my abandonment very slowly and unconsciously. I got fewer hugs… There was no strong male presence to provide feelings of nurturing and safety. I think I shut down little by little. Then at age twenty when my mother died, I was done with feeling… period. Now as I sat in the therapist office, something broke me open and I was sinking into a deep grief over the loss of my parents – in my mid 40's!

My therapist gave me the language for my behavior. But he didn't offer any tools for healing. I spent the next six months crying for hours, every day. I would sit in my big office hoping no one would stop by to talk to me.

One evening during this dark period, I stayed late at the office. I went to the copy machine to grab some documents and found a poem on the platen. The poem is titled Desiderate by Max Ehrmann. In some ways, this poem may have saved my life.

The first line *"Go placidly amid the noise and haste, and remember what peace there may be in silence"* felt like an invitation. It had not occurred to me tobe silent. My left brain didn't like silence. But I soon discovered that in the silence, I could access my deepest feelings – something I sensed was important if I wanted to heal.

Another favorite line gave me a perspective on my tendency to be very judgmental of myself and others. *"If you compare yourself with others, you may become vain and bitter; for always there will be greater and lesser persons than yourself."* And finally, the line that felt like I was being given permission to heal and thrive was you have a right to be here. *"And whether or not it is clear to you, no doubt the universe is unfolding as it should."*

I read this poem several times a day for months. Finally, the grief started to lift. I began to feel some relief. I felt like I was emerging from a heavy cloud. I even felt a little joy. I started to sense an inner guidance – something I named 'my indelible identity', that part of me that could not be destroyed no matter what. It was the beginning of a long journey of learning to love myself.

My Healing Journey

Being generous with our attention and praise requires us to feel good about ourselves. This is not always easy. My healing journey took many years and through some very difficult places.

As a young adult, I felt very lost and unsure of myself most of the time. I took other people's comments and actions very personally. I always looked outside myself for validation. I often felt hurt as a result. As I've grown and healed many of my early traumas, I can hear negative comments and view them objectively. I feel that the more we heal and learn to love ourselves, the more we realize that many hurtful comments are just the projections of other people's insecurities.

Over the years, I have tried many psychological healing modalities. There are various ways to heal trauma and negative patterns from our childhood and beyond. I have concluded that there are a couple of techniques that work very well. And these techniques are simple and available to do alone or with a friend.

> *"Life will give you whatever experience is most helpful for your evolution of consciousness."* – Eckhart Tolle

Our Thoughts Create Our Reality

In my mid-20s, I had a life-changing experience. I spent two intense weekends in the EST Training (Erhard Seminar Training). In the training, I received three huge insights. 1) I get to choose my experience. In other words, I am never a victim. I always have a choice in my reactions to every situation or event in my life. 2) Every feeling or emotion is affected by an earlier experience. So, if we ask ourselves, "When have I felt this emotion before?" we can often get to the root of the trauma or destructive feeling or emotion. 3) There is a creative force in the Universe. Some call it God. I had given up on God at that point. So, I regained my sense of connection to a creative force.

Positive Affirmations

Fortified by my new insights, I set out to live my life. Even with my greatest efforts, I still felt insecure and self-loathing. If anyone tried to get emotionally close to me, I would push them away. If someone paid me a compliment, I would diminish their comment. I was unable to hear anything good about myself. One day I heard the Groucho Marx quote, "I would never belong to a club that would have someone like me as a member." I immediately felt the truth in that for me…

After years of searching for answers, I stumbled across a powerful technique that transformed mylife. I attended a lecture on the power of positive affirmations. The speaker suggested that a majority of our emotions and reactions are based on messages we heard or experiences we had during our childhood. These messages and experiences influenced us unconsciously or emerged as self-talk and internal dialog.

The speaker suggested overwriting all negative unconscious beliefs and negative self-talk with positive affirmations. He claimed that 30 days of saying positive affirmations several times a daywould totally rewire our brains. This seemed very logical to me. And I love logical solutions. So, I decided to try it.

The next week, I went to a spiritual bookstore and picked up a cassette tape called "Feeling Fine Affirmations" by Louise Hay. When I listened to it, I thought it seemed a little silly. On the recording, Louise repeated phrases like "I love myself. You love yourself. My friends love me. Your friends love you. My coworkers love me. Your coworkers love you." And it went on and on. Plus, the background music was repetitive and boring. But I was determined to test this theory. So, I decided to listen to the affirmations while I was falling asleep. This worked beautifully!

Each night, I set the cassette player on a repeating loop. I would fall asleep and stay asleep for several hours while the positive affirmations went deep into my subconscious. After a few weeks, I started to notice a difference. I was no longer reacting to people the way I usually did. I was much less defensive. I noticed that I didn't get triggered as easily. I started feeling more confident. I was really surprised at the difference. I felt that I had found the magic formula. Healing my psyche while I slept was the perfect solution for me.

Energy Healing

Inspired by my emerging strength, I began to look for ways to help my family. My husband and I decided to move to the Philadelphia area to shorten my commute and live near family.

My career advanced quite rapidly in the Philadelphia area. I worked for several different financial services organizations and eventually started my own consulting business. I also took on a huge and scary endeavor. I decided to write a book. Since my knowledge was in high demand, I easily found a publisher. Nine months later I completed first book, Data Mining Cookbook (Wiley 2001).

The publication of my new book catapulted me to the world stage. I was speaking and teaching at different conferences several times a month for the next few years. I thought I had it all under control.

I never imagined myself getting cancer. After my mother died of cancer, I was determined that it would never happen to me. In my early 20s, my severe health issues resulting from my car accident sparked a lifelong passion for nutrition I decided to eat only organic foods and drink pure water. I tooknumerous supplements. I had some sort of false confidence that I would never get cancer. But the stress of taking care of everyone to my own neglect was my downfall. In 1999, I was diagnosed with breast cancer.

I clearly remember the doctor telling me I had a nine- centimeter tumor. I was shocked and a bit frightened. I don't think the seriousness of my situation had hit me yet… I immediately asked what I needed to do to get through it.

The next thing I knew, I was scheduling an emergency mastectomy and reconstructive surgery. I sat down with my wonderful oncologist and scheduled my chemotherapy so that I could maintain my travel and speaking schedule. I knew if I kept planning for the future, I could maintain my positive attitude.

To balance the toxicity of the chemotherapy, my Integrative Medicine doctor started me on vitamin IVs twice a week. This intense nutrition helped me maintain my energy. So, I never missed a scheduled event over the entire six months of chemotherapy and radiation.

Finally, I was done with all my treatments. Now I had to determine what was out of balance in my life that allowed this cancer to grow in the first place. I realized that I was surviving on adrenaline. When I considered how close I came to dying, it scared me. My mother died at the same age, probably because she was taking care of everyone else. I suddenly realized that I was following in her footsteps. When I mentioned it to my doctor, he suggested I see a therapist to work on my emotional patterns. The next week, I met with Julie Roberts and was introduced to an energy healing technique called CLEAR®.

To say that I was resistant to energy healing is an understatement. After all, I was a data scientist. My leftbrain ruled. I had years of psychotherapy. And I could not accept the fact that I held trauma in my energy body that prevented me from fully healing and loving myself.

I completed Julie's weekend CLEAR® training at least six times over the next four years. And I still resisted the fact that it worked. Then one morning I was preparing to teach a predictive modeling course at a major training center. I was suddenly paralyzed with fear. I knew that the people who attended my class in this particular city could be very harsh in their evaluations. I was dreading teaching the class for fear of receiving poor evaluations. I was desperate.

I decided to test the CLEAR® technique on myself. I used kinesiology to determine the energy points to clear. I felt into the fear and stayed with it for a few minutes. Suddenly it disappeared. I have no other explanation for my experience. I felt totally different. The fear was gone.

I headed to the class room and taught one of mybest classes ever. My students gave me glowing reviews. That was the day I truly embraced the power of CLEAR®. I still use the CLEAR® method almost every day.

You will find more information on the CLEAR® method in the Resources section of the Appendix.

Seeds of Self-Love

After many years of deep inner work and healing, I find myself being very curious about other people's journeys and how their own level of self-love affects their ability to be successful.

I recently attended a conference celebrating the power of women called "The World-Changing Women's Conference." The first evening, 300+ women gathered to enjoy a deeply moving panel discussion. Four brave women displayed incredible courage as they shared personal stories of major business and political failure. Their honesty and vulnerability were truly inspiring. Each of them shared their grief around the loss of their dream. At the same time, they were all on a path towards a new dream.

As I marveled at their courage, I found myself wanting to learn more about these women. After such monumental failures, why were they able to pick themselves up and try again? Why were they able to learn from her mistakes and move on while many of us might give up? What made them different?

As I pondered this question over the next several weeks, I realized a pattern. Each of these women appeared to have a deep understanding of themselves. They seemed to believe in themselves at some core level. They also described having strong support systems through family and friends. This combination of self-knowing, self-respect, and a loving support system seemed to give them the confidence to pick themselves up and try again. Many of us are not so lucky.

"Nobody will love you until you love yourself." – The Dalai Lama

Our earliest imprints of connection and safety, both emotional and physical, come from our relationship with our mother. According to Thomas Lewis, M.D., Fari Amini, M.D., Richard Lannon, M.D. in "A General Theory of Love", the kind of mother we have predicts our emotional traits later in life. "Consistently attentive, responsive and tender mothers raise a secure child who uses his mother as a safe haven from which to explore the world. Later, they were happy, socially competent, resilient, persistent and likable grade-schoolers who were empathic with others. A cold, resentful, rigid mother produces an insecure-avoidant child who becomes distant, hostile to authority, shuns togetherness and won't ask for comfort. A mother distracted or erratic in her attentions raises an insecure-ambivalent toddler, clutching when together and wailing when apart who later becomes socially inept, timid, hypersensitive and lacking confidence. Attachment security is a powerful predictor of life success."

In the article, "*Being a Witness to Our Suffering,*" Julie Roberts Ph.D. explains, *"As children, when our pain is not seen, it is traumatic and we often end up questioning if there is something wrong with us. We can even think we are crazy because we feel so much and no one else sees how difficult things are for us. Children need acknowledgment of what they feel. When they don't get it, it is likely they will end up repeating a dramatic pattern in an attempt to get those unfulfilled needs met or they will begin to self- medicate to numb themselves to those feelings."*

So many of us may feel that there is something wrong with us. As we gain an understanding of the underlying causes, we learn to be more understanding and compassionate with ourselves.

Practices for Self-Healing and Self-Love

The following are some suggestions and practices that I use in my daily healing process. I invite you to try them out for yourself. Think of these practices as creating new neural pathways. With a little consistency, you will literally be rewiring your brain!

Deep Breathing

Many spiritual teachings focus on the breath. Deep breathing is such a powerful tool for healing with so many benefits. When preparing for meditation or just wanting to calm your nerves, taking a few deep breaths can work wonders. See if you can pull your breath all the way into your abdomen. Hold it for a moment before releasing. Feel your body and mind relax.

Meditation

Meditation is the practice of relaxing and quieting your mind. As thoughts, images and other sensations enter your mind, your goal is to not give them your attention. If you are new to meditation, I encourage you to seek out a teacher or research techniques that work for you. A daily meditation practice has so many benefits. Your ability to better control your thoughts and habits is very powerful on your healing journey.

Contemplation

Contemplation is a practice of focus. I feel that it gives us access to our higher guidance. If you are working with a particular issue or goal, this practice can be very revealing. Begin with a few minutes of meditation. Then immerse yourself with your object of contemplation until you feel yourself becoming one with it. Images and strings of ideas and thoughts will enter your mind, revealing deep insights and higher truths about your object of contemplation.

Morning Writing

Each morning upon awakening and before you engage your brain, start writing. Imagine your soul or higher self wants to tell you something. Don't think about what you are writing. Just let it flow. If you feel blocked, just write two or three sentences about how you don't know what to write. If you consistently make the effort, it will finally start to flow. It may take a few days or a week. If you do this every morning, I think you will be amazed by what eventually comes through.

Appreciation and Gratitude

Whenever something goes wrong or you get frustrated, think about how much good you have in your life. If I have a bad day, I start thinking about my blessings. I live in a safe neighborhood. I have a comfortable home, good food, wonderful family and friends. Compared to most of the world, most of us live in paradise.

Self-Compassion and Forgiveness

Pay attention to things you say to yourself, especially when you feel that you made a mistake. This is a great opportunity to remember the words of Matt Kahn. He basically says that in any situation, "You deserve more LOVE not less."

I like to think that I am always doing my best. And I'm trying to get better. That allows me to be gentle with myself when I do something that I later regret.

Loving Language

I like to use positive words as much as possible. Some research suggests that the brain doesn't retain negating words. So, it's always more effective to speak in positives. For example, you might want someone close to you to stop interrupting you. Instead of saying, "Please stop interrupting me!" you might say, "Please let me complete my sentence!"

It reinforces the positive action rather than focusing on the word "Interrupt."

One of my pet peeves is the phrase "No Problem." This phrase is very common in the workplace. When someone says this phrase often, our mind forgets the 'No' and remembers that person in association with the word "Problem." That might not be what we want. I try to say "Quite okay" instead. It leaves the listener with a more positive feeling.

Another common word that has devastating effects on a conversation is the word "but." Let's say we're in a conversation in which someone shares their opinion. If we want to add our thoughts, we might say we agree and then use the word 'but' which negates our statement of agreement. If we use the word 'and' we can value their comments while introducing some new ideas.

Final Thoughts

Loving all of yourself is foundational for showing up powerfully and sharing your gifts. As you progress through the chapters, you might feel overwhelmedor resistant. This is just more data revealing that you should love more of yourself. This step takes time. Be patient with yourself and trust the process.

Reflections

As you reflect on my healing journey, did you notice any similarities to experiences in your own life? Have you felt abandonment in one form or another? Did you suffer from abuse or bullying? We you traumatized in other ways? Even though it often feels like it, know that you are not alone...

Very few of us grow up without some sort of wounding. I think of these experiences as the fine- tuning needed to prepare us to step into our Inspired Purpose. Our strength, humility, and wisdom are gained and refined as we bravely face our greatest challenges.

Once you commit to your healing journey, amazing miracles will show up in your life. You will meet others who are on the path of healing and stepping into their greatness. You will inspire each other. You will begin to discover your Superpowers. You will feel lighter, more joyful, and ready to step into your Inspired Purpose. Trust the process.

Chapter 4
Own Your Superpowers

"Our deepest fear is not that we are inadequate. Our deepest fear is that we are powerful beyond measure. It is our light, not our darkness that most frightens us. We ask ourselves, Who am I to be brilliant, gorgeous, talented, and fabulous?
Actually, who are you not to be? You are a child; you're playing small does not serve the world. There is nothing enlightened about shrinking so that other people will not feel insecure around you. We are all meant to shine, as children do. We were born to make manifest the glory of God that is within us. It is not just in some of us; it is in everyone and as we let our own light shine, we unconsciously give others permission to do the same. As we are liberated from our own fear, our presence automatically liberates others." - Marianne Williamson, A Return to Love (Permission to share the full poem granted by the Marianne Williamson Team July 2018*)*

I love this quote by Marianne Williamson. I remember the first time I read it. I felt a huge sense of relief coming over me.

I initially read this quote as I was gaining recognition for my first book. I was starting to get lots of invitations to speak and teach at major data conferences around the world. And while the acknowledgment felt good, deep down I was terrified.

As I read this quote, I realized that I had a fear of being seen. At first, I didn't know why. But I was definitely struggling to stay small in my work and life. As I thought about my childhood, I realized it was a pattern I had developed at a very young age.

After my father died, my mother began working long hours. What had been a fairly stable home life turned to a life of drama and chaos. To feel safe, I became invisible.

Landing a job in the corporate world was such a blessing in disguise. But it was never easy. After six months of building successful predictive models for a small innovative credit card bank, I was promoted to Head of Acquisition. In my new position, I was in charge of operations as well as marketing for the bank's two major credit cards. I was now expected to lead six talented people who managed huge complex areas of their own. I was so over my head, it wasn't funny. I was terrified. I only stayed because my husband's business was barely making it. So, I had to maintain my income. Every day I buried my fear and acted as if I knew what I was doing.

Dealing with overwhelming fear was a constant battle. Every day I struggled to reconcile my work life with my spiritual life. One day out of desperation, I made a decision to change my thoughts. I took a deep breath and put my attention on my heart. Almost immediately, I felt a sense of calm come over me. I even felt a very unfamiliar sense of joy. This experience was so powerful that I made a promise to myself to be in my heart as much as possible. This practice helped me relax. I also felt more at ease, even in difficult conversations. Plus, I noticed people began to respond to me differently. I didn't realize it at the time, but when I intentionally communicated with a focus on my heart energy, others were positively affected.

I later discovered that when I connected with others and communicated from my heart, they often reflected that they felt inspired. I didn't realize it at the time but this is one of my Superpowers. I feel that heart-centered communication is a Superpower we all can master. And it can have a long-term positive impact, especially in the corporate world.

The Wounded Healer

"your unique gift is related with your deepest trauma. In this journey to come to your calling, throughout life, you will be pushed and pulled in the direction of what your deepest trauma is about. In that you will find your unique diamond." – Ria Baeck

Many of us who yearn to create a career and life of inspired purpose are wounded healers. Our early wounding hones our compassion and our empathy. So, as adults we tend to want to alleviate the suffering of others. We want to make a positive difference in the world because we understand that we are all in this together. But many of us have not yet embraced our own Superpowers. Our wounds keep us small and silent. **It is through the healing of our wounds**

that we gain compassion for ourselves and others. As we heal, we often awaken our deepest yearnings and discover our unique gifts or Superpowers.

My own healing process unveiled another one of my Superpowers - my ability to inspire. I love inspiring others to step into their greatness. I would love the opportunity to do more of this.

I first discovered this ability a few months after joining the marketing team at a large credit card bank. This new bank was being acquired by the bank I just left. So, I knew both banks very well – especially their cultures.

As my coworkers learned about my experience at the acquiring bank, they came to me for advice. Many of them were afraid and wanted some to know what it might be like to work for this new bank. Since all of our marketing efforts were halted, I spent most of my day coaching people. Fortunately, the acquiring bank had a great culture. So, I spent most of my time inspiring people to tap into what they wanted to do and bring out their greatest talents.

After a few weeks, I realized how much happier I felt at the end of a long work day. I knew I had tapped into some innate gift within me. I knew that inspiring others was a gift I wanted to share in service to the greater good.

Feminine Rising

Corporate America is not exactly known for embracing or encouraging feminine qualities.

However, research suggests that successful CEOs, regardless of gender, state that they trust their intuition – a more feminine gift.

In a Harvard Business Review article entitled "When to Trust your Gut", Alden M. Hayashi states, "I found that recent research has uncovered some striking clues suggesting that our emotions and feelings might not only be important in our intuitive ability to make good decisions but may actually be essential. Furthermore, I was told, the type of instinctive genius that enables a CEO to craft the perfect strategy for usurping competitors could require an uncanny ability to detect patterns, perhaps subconsciously, that other people either overlook or mistake for randomnoise."

What I love about this research is that it highlights another important point. Feminine power is not only available to and important for women, but men will benefit from embracing their more feminine qualities. Our creativity as well as our ability to connect and empathize all emerge from our feminine aspects. In fact, this balance of the masculine and feminine is essential for empowering us to bring love into business.

Keys to Our Superpowers

We all have Superpowers that go unnoticed, even by us. These innate talents are what allow us to share our gifts with the world. As you think back over your life, notice where you felt inspired as you shared your inspired talents. Those memories are the clues to your Superpowers.

Below, I've listed some common roles that these Superpowers frequently are used in. See if any of these qualities are natural to you:

- Empathic (nurse, childcare worker, hospice worker, leader)
- Good listener (psychotherapist, coach,hospice worker)
- See potential greatness in others (teacher, coach, manager, leader)
- System thinker (CEO, engineer, politician)
- Intuitive and sensitive (healer, coach, artist)
- Good problem solver (analyst, consultant)
- Artistically gifted (artist, musician, designer)

Another way of unveiling a Superpower is to thinkof a trait that we consider negative. For example, we may feel like we are impatient. By looking at the situation from a different perspective, our impatience might mean that we grasp things quickly. We are a quick study. This perspective can give us more confidence in our abilities and perhaps the grace to be patient with others.

Let me share how I was able to tap into a couple of my Superpowers and how you can too.

I Am a Writer

When I first declared my Superpower of writing, I felt a gripping in my gut. I still find it hard to claim that I am a writer. 30 years ago, if you had told me I would be writing books for a living I would have replied, "You are crazy. I can barely read!"

As a kid, I was very curious. I loved anything having to do with art and puzzles. But I had trouble concentrating. I couldn't read books of any length. Instead, I fed my curiosity with short stories and encyclopedias. I also enjoyed math. So, if I wanted the chance to have at a successful career, math seemed like the logical area of study.

Several years after getting a degree in math, I embarked on my own healing journey. In an effort to understand myself, I became very curious about human nature. So, I started taking graduate courses in psychology.

Over the next few years, I began searching for more ways to heal and gain deeper meaning in my life. I remember going to monthly gatherings at our community center where a gentleman would lead us in guided meditations. At one of these events, this gentleman said he was going to lead us through a visualization where we would be guided to ask a question. I was feeling lost and aimless in my life. Our household still had money problems. I wanted deeper insights into myself and my life path.

We closed our eyes and the facilitator guided us through a beautiful garden, then into the forest. At the end of the forest path, we encountered a wizard. We were instructed to ask the wizard a question. So, in my mind, I asked the wizard, "What am I supposed to do with my life?" He said one word, "Write!" It was another 15 years before I began to embrace this Superpower.

I Am a Systems Thinker

As someone who loves to solve problems, I now view the world as a giant puzzle. **In today's complex world, having the ability to see the big picture is valuable.**

But with the deluge of informationcoming into our awareness every day, **the ability to feel, sense, or intuit is quickly becoming even more valuable.**

As a data scientist, I use my left brain to solve linear problems. But my right brain is where I discern non- linear relationships, connect patterns, and filter out the noise to reveal what is truly important. It was this ability to make connections and see the big picture that led to my realization that love could transform the corporate world and be vehicles for positive change in the world.

Early in my corporate career, I attended many high- level business meetings where I never said a word. I was comfortable in one-on-one conversations. But in a group, I was paralyzed with fear. At the time, I didn't understand why. I imagine it was desire to remain invisible. However, the success of my career depended on my ability to share in front of groups.

In the mid-90s, my husband's health was deteriorating. So, our family decided to move to the East coast to be near family. The credit card bank set up a transfer to their insurance division just outside of Philadelphia. It was a gift in so many ways.

In contrast to the credit card bank, the culture at the insurance division was much more loving. I was still very shy and afraid to be visible. Luckily, I had a wonderful manager who insisted I take a Dale Carnegie course.

The course was brilliant. Each week we learned a new skill and were required to give a 5-minute presentation. The culture was designed to make us feel very safe and appreciated, no matter how badly we performed. During the first few classes, I was petrified. But slowly I began to feel safe and tap into some of the joy of sharing my truth with others. I also discovered one of my Superpowers. I'm able to think on my feet and create a heart connection with my audience.

Over the next few years, I worked for several financial institutions. I experienced numerous mergers and acquisitions. During each transition, **I saw how people suffered and by extension, how profits suffered. Everyone was so afraid for their security that people started to protect their own turf. In some situations, the work culture became downright hostile. Communication, compassion, and connection disappeared.**

The shift in culture was very challenging for me. As a data scientist, I focused on numbers and patterns. But in my personal life, I was a passionate spiritual seeker. This polarity created tension in my psyche.

I clearly remember a day when I was struggling with these two, seemingly opposite, aspects of my life. In my meditation, I asked the question, "Why am I stuck in the corporate world? I hate the fear-based culture. I feel like my soul is dying." The answer I heard was, "This is where you need to be to learn the skills to do your real work!" I had no idea what that meant. I would learn the answer some ten years later.

At the same time, I started getting noticed for my work in data science – specifically predictive modeling. I was invited to speak at numerous data conferences around the world. I always gave at least one presentation on predictive modeling. But many times, I would suggest presentations on other topics such as good communication skills, the importance of creativity, and how to manage change. I felt much more passion around these topics. But I still felt that I had to keep it separate from my statistical work.

Then, as I mentioned earlier, I read "The World is Flat" by Thomas Freeman. I was so intrigued by Freeman's revelations that I got the audio book and listened to it three times. The gist of the book is that technology is changing the way we do business. The world is going global, digital, and virtual, a fact that changes the very nature of what drives success.

Then I had one of those 'Aha!' moments. I realized that if the world is going global, digital, and virtual, we all need to be more agile and resilient in our businesses. This cannot be accomplished in a fear-based, top-down, hierarchical corporate structure. If the market changes quickly, businesses must adapt quickly as well. In fact, the most successful companies are agile and resilient enough to actually disrupt the market – forcing everyone else to quickly adapt!

This connection brought my worlds together. I could see howthe combination of technology and big data was driving rapid changes in the global marketplace. And that companies who evolved their culture of fear into a culture of empowerment and caring would be more successful.

This led to the writing of my second book, Business Intelligence Success Factors, Aligning for Success in a Global Economy (Wiley/SAS, 2009).

Making this connection also gave me a sense of my real work. I began integrating the language of communication and connection into all my talks – even those with a statistical focus. I communicated at this level for several years as I kept going deeper, trying to unveil the bigger pattern. I know now that it relates to my Inspired Purpose of bringing love into the corporate world. But it would be a few more years before the bigger picture emerged.

This process of discovery allowed me to recognize another of my Superpowers – systems thinking – the ability to see many parts as a system. In other words, I have the ability to see how events connect and interrelate. When something happens that seems surprising or unexpected, I can often identify at least one underlying cause. And I can often see both sides of an argument and where there might be common ground or overlapping interests.

This ability also helped me to evolve my business skills. While my work consisted of writing programs to develop predictive models, I began to notice that software companies were building automated predictive modeling tools. At first, I was concerned.I thought that my skills might become obsolete. Then I realized that I could leverage my systems thinking abilities to build more powerful predictive models through unique data structuring, the creative use of weights, and optimizing implementation strategies. I also had more time to help the business stakeholders understand and embrace predictive analytics by showing them the benefits to the bottom line. **Both my creativity and communication skills were enhanced by my ability to communicate with my heart as well as my head. Now I feel inspired to help others balance their left-brain thinking with an open heart. As shared in Chapter 1, the benefits go way beyond the bottom line.**

Being of Service

"Every day, think as you wake up, today I am fortunate to be alive, I have a precious human life, I am not going to waste it. I am going to use all my energies to develop myself, to expand my heart out to others; to achieve enlightenment for the benefit of all beings. I am going to have kind thoughts towards others, I am not going to get angry or think badly about others. I am going to benefit others as much as I can." - The Dalai Lama

Many aspects of our modern culture encourage us to feel that we are in competition with each other – for everything. A majority of corporate advertising is designed to make us feel diminished if we don't have the best car, the biggest house, or the trendiest clothes. And we can clearly see the dissatisfaction this creates. Just look at the level of drug addiction, reliance on antidepressants, and self- destructive behavior in our communities. It's obvious that our cultural model isn't healthy for many people. And it is also out of alignment with many spiritual teachings.

So, what is it we yearn for? What do all these material possessions replace?

We yearn to fully step into the one we are meant to become. We yearn to be truly seen, heard, and valued for our gifts – gifts that are most often shared in service to others.

Buddhism speaks of "the path of awakening" that "points to the importance of serving a context larger than one's self."

Buddhist teachings also suggest that if we reach a stage of awakened consciousness, we are "blessed with many Super Human abilities." The teachings go on to say, "It is literally built into the fabric of the universe that one cannot reliably get access to these Super Human abilities unless they are committed to a context larger than themselves."

In Chapter 2, we saw how the evolution of consciousness eventually requires us to transcend our ego. Ultimately, we are invited to 'Awaken' to who we truly are – spiritual beings having a human experience. From a soul perspective, many spiritual teachings suggest that we chose to incarnate at this time to be in service to planetary awakening. So not only are we invited to show up and serve. **From a soul perspective, it's our obligation to show up, share our gifts, and serve the greater good.**

If we set the intention to serve others, I feel that our gifts or Superpowers will easily emerge. As we look at our interconnected world, it is becoming increasingly apparent that we need each other to reach our greatest expression of our innate talents and wisdom. This concept is also supported by many spiritual traditions.

If you don't feel drawn to being in service to others on a grand scale, experiment with being in service in small ways. Offer a kind word to someone or spend some time deeply listening to a friend. There are many small ways to be in service to others. Sometimes it's just a matter of setting the intention and noticing.

Final Thoughts

The act of unveiling and embracing your Superpowers is essential for Visualizing Your Inspired Purpose. If you feel any shyness or fear of discovering your greatness, go back to Chapter 3 and see if you can find more ways to Love All of Yourself.

Reflections

Set aside a few minutes each evening to reflect on your day. When did you feel happy? What were you doing? Did you have an experience of losing track of time? Notice what you were doing. What actions did you take that helped others? These are all clues to your Superpowers.

Chapter 5
Visualize Your Inspired Purpose

As you think about your Inspired Purpose – your "reason for being" so to speak – how does it line up with your current career? For many of us, our career is based on needs or desires that are driven by unconscious beliefs and patterns. We may be a doctor because that was what our parents told us to become. Or we squashed our desire to be an artist because we were led to believe we would always be poor. So, we got an MBA instead. Many of these decisions bring financial success. But they rarely leave us feeling satisfied, let alone inspired.

"It's official.
There is room in the Universe for you to dream bigger.
Go ahead, blow God's mind." – Matt Kahn

I feel that we were all born with an Inspired Purpose. Some call it our Soul Purpose. In this chapter, I invite you to explore deep within yourself and see what inspires you. We will look at how your values relate to your Inspired Purpose. **We will also look at what might be holding you back from stepping into your Inspired Purpose. As we use several techniques to delve into this exploration, we might discover places where we need to love ourselves more. Or we might reveal more Superpowers. It's all expected along the path to unveiling our Inspired Purpose.**

As evidenced by my personal stories so far, it's clear that my path to finding my Inspired Purpose has been long and arduous. And I've taken many detours. As I heal and work to Love All of Myself and Own My Superpowers, my path towards visualizing and fulfilling my Inspired Purpose gets easier. The writing of this book is a big step towards living my Inspired Purpose.

My hope is that by sharing my journey, your path towards your Inspired Purpose will more direct and easier than mine. Just know that however long the journey, it is worth it. I'm confident that as you move towards your own Inspired Purpose, unique insights will emerge. You will begin to access your deeper wisdom. You will experience joy just being on the path because after all, it was what you came here to do.

In the previous chapter, I shared how my Superpower as a Systems Thinker revealed itself many years ago. By studying multiple patterns, I realized that an organization's ability to be agile and resilient in our high-tech global economy is enabled by a corporate culture that values human competencies such as compassion, connection, and caring. Over the next few years, I was invited to speak at numerous data conferences. While the conference organizers were interested in my data science expertise, I was more interested in sharing my insights on the importance of the human competencies as drivers of success. I proposed presentations on effective communication, collaboration, creativity, and authentic leadership. These topics were a big hit with attendees. And when I was presenting on these topics, I felt like I was totally in flow. ***That's when it hit me! As we embrace our Superpowers and step into our Inspired Purpose, we step into our flow – the birthplace of joy and creativity.***

Many years later, I realized that my Inspired Purpose was to bring these concepts to the corporate world. But my path wasn't clear. So, I continued to work as a data scientist while I refined my message. ***Now I am clear and ready to share my message – to show that Love is the greatest driver of success in business today.***

Paths to Your Purpose

"There is no coming to consciousness without pain. People will do anything, no matter how absurd, in order to avoid facing their own soul. One does not become enlightened by imagining figures of light but by making the darkness conscious." – Carl Gustav Jung; Alchemical Studies, Collected Works Vol.13, par 335, p.265

As we Own Our Superpowers, our Inspired Purpose may emerge easily. That is the beauty of taking time to heal and understand our powers and desires. However, sometimes we need to attract adversity to allow our Inspired Purpose to reveal itself.

The Cosmic 2x4

"Then there is the paradox of the Soul actually using trauma to wake us up to the deeper reality of a loving living Universe. The trauma can be seen as having hidden lessons of 'growth and awakening'." – Antanas Vainius

As I shared earlier, I spent a lot of my life feeling like a victim. When I realized that each and every tragedy happened for my benefit, I got very clear that their purpose was to wake me up. Each time, I felt like I was being hit by a Cosmic 2x4.

With my new realization, I knew I didn't need any more Cosmic 2x4s. And I sure didn't want any more. I knew I was ready to make a change – ready to livea more intentional life. I told the Universe that I was going to dedicate my life to finding and living my Inspired Purpose. I was going to dedicate my life to being of service to something greater than myself.

Our Great Hunger

"Your soul's calling might be shining through since childhood or it may only appear later in adulthood, but at some point, in time there is a calling that is so deep and so compelling to you, that you just have to pay attention."
– Rhea Beck

In "The Awakened Woman", Tererai Trent invites you to "discover and call out your sacred dream, your Great Hunger." She invites us to ask ourselves this simple question: *"What breaks my heart?"*

She continues, "Let this question be like a heartbeat: as you wash dishes, rock your child to sleep, commute to work, walk the dog, and breathe in and out, allow this question to pulse within you…"

"When you watch the news or when you think about the state of the world today: *What breaks your heart?*" Tererai beckons. "Forever, your Great Hunger continues to call you to become the person you were always meant to be, to reach your full potential, and to heal yourself by caring for your community, even if you're not sure exactly who that person is or how to do it."

I strongly resonate with Tererai's question, *"What breaks your heart?"* On my journey towards my Inspired Purpose, I saw how large corporations greedily consumed our precious natural resources and left pollution in its place. This broke my heart. I saw how corporations failed to value their human capital. This broke my heart. It took me many years to understand how my expertise in data science, my interest in emotional intelligence, and my spiritual journey would all coalesce to blossom into an argument for bringing love into business.

Accessing Your Higher Guidance

One way to think about our Inspired Purpose is in relation to what our ancestors yearn for us to do. In her amazing book "The Ancient Ones Are Calling Us," Sue Cimino shares her exciting adventure of bringing healing to the other side of the planet – Tasmania. By trusting and following her higher guidance, Sue reveals how her Inspired Purpose is unveiled.

Sue found that she connected deeply with the trauma of many indigenous and aboriginal peoples who had been treated horribly for hundreds of years. Her connection to the land and water brought her close to their enduring Spirit. She learned that her Inspired Purpose was to bring healing to their Spirit.

Sue shares her beautiful perspective on our Inspired Purpose.

"We all come into this world encoded like a seed . . . with our blueprint, what we are here for, what our gifts are, what we can become. Look at the oak tree, whose template is fully held inside the acorn. It is just waiting for the right conditions to express its full oak-tree self. We are the same. Within each one of us is a deep memory of our essence, what we're designed for, and what will fulfill us like nothing else.

The oak tree doesn't suffer self-doubt or criticize itself for being what it is. It doesn't compare itself to others and feel not good enough. Or wail that it doesn't know how to grow into a tree. It wears its oak leaves with certainty as it slowly grows into an enormous and beautiful tree, a full expression of its divine design.

Within every seed and within each one of us, is the urge, the whisper, that inclination . . . Showing us the direction, the path to the fulfillment of our destiny . . . Whether we recognize it or not."

– Sue Cimino, with permission, *"The Ancient Ones are Calling Us"*

Sue continues with her guidance from our ancestors. She beckons us to become the stewards of this new consciousness.

"You are the seed of the new being. You are not the fruit — it is not time for you to decay — it's time for you to blossom. You can do more than you know. The ancestors will work with you and through you. Do not doubt yourself or them. We have waited a long time for you to be ready. There are others too, coming of age. All of Creation is supporting you. The ground is ready — the ground of consciousness. Your fertile ground is in consciousness. Yes, it's true — be the gardener in consciousness" – The Ancient Ones

– Sue Cimino, with permission, "*The Ancient Ones are Calling Us*"

Based on Sue's guidance and many other spiritual teachers, it is not just for our own satisfaction that we commit to our Inspired Purpose. I would argue that it is our obligation. Our conscious evolution needs every one of us to become who we were born to be. No exceptions!

Aligning with Your Passions

Once you commit to discovering your Inspired Purpose, life can open up in miraculous ways. One way to discover your Purpose is to spend time exploring your passions.

According to Janet Bray Attwood and Chris Attwood, creators of The Passion Test®, successful people know their top 5 passions and always follow this simple rule. "*When you are faced with a choice, a decision, or an opportunity, choose in favor of your passions."*

Janet and Chris suggest that our passions are signposts that lead us to our inspired purpose. I encourage you to visit their website and take The Passion Test®. Their highly refined process helps you prioritize your passions and measure how closely your life is aligned with your passions.

They offer great strategies for staying focused on your passions and discovering your Inspired Purpose.

Living an Inspired Life

Another powerful technique for unveiling your Inspired Purpose is to create your own list of Personal Values. In Chapter 1, we learned about some inspiring Corporate Values statements for 'loving' companies. Just like how these statements become guides for how companies operate, declaring your Personal Values can help to clarify your Inspired Purpose. As you consider how you want to show up in the world and share your unique gifts, this is a great next step.

Personal Values Declaration

A personal values declaration is a clear and specific list or statement that declares what traits or behaviors are most important to you. In many ways, they reveal what we care about. Our values make us unique and serve as our guide, especially in difficult times. When we are true to our values, we are happier and more successful. When we are not true to our values, we often lose our way and end up feeling unhappy or depressed.

Looking at the Values of some of our greatest leaders can inspire our own thinking. One of my favorites is Ben Franklin.

While the wording of Ben Franklin's governing values may seem a little old fashioned, I feel that their underlying power is why he had so many amazing accomplishments in his lifetime.

Here's a sample of a few I like:

- Temperance: Eat not to dullness; drink not to elevation.
- Silence: Speak not but what may benefit others or yourself; avoid trifling conversation.

- Resolution: Resolve to perform what you ought; perform without fail what you resolve.

Can you see the relevance of these values in your life? He values a balanced lifestyle in which one only engages in meaningful conversations. And he values a strong work ethic with great resolve to complete what he started – still powerful today.

While I agree with all of Ben Franklin's values, I define my values using more global language:

- **Love** – interacting with all beings from a place of open-heartedness which encompasses compassion, empathy, kindness, patience, trust, forgiveness, and seeing the best in everyone.

- **Wisdom** – honoring and blending knowledge, keen observation, insight, experience, critical thinking, and higher guidance or intuition.

- **Integrity** – striving for wholeness, respect, honesty, reliability, accountability, and dependability.

- **Stewardship** – honoring and caring for all life and the natural world.

- **Joy** – being content and grateful for every experience.

I am still working on living in full alignment with my values. I know I come up short in areas. Sometimes I get angry with people who seem to be abusing their power in the world. I deal with my upset by staying informed as well as sending loving thoughts their way.

I also share my values with trusted friends and family. I ask them to lovingly reflect back to me when they feel I am in alignment with my values and when I am not.

Now that I've declared my Personal Values, I'm ready to create my Inspired Life Plan to support my life of Inspired Purpose.

Inspired Life Plan

"What would you set aside, put down, let go of in order to create a space within as wide as the star-lit sky for what your soul desires?"
– Oriah Mountain Dreamer

Your Inspired Life Plan serves as a roadmap for living your life of Inspired Purpose. It is a living breathing plan that invites you to refine and revise it as your path evolves and new insights and desires emerge.

Your Inspired Life Plan consists of a few steps that are designed to help you gain clarity around the characteristics of your ideal life. We begin by making a list of the characteristics that represent our ideal living situation that supports you in stepping into your Inspired Purpose.

Creating Your Inspired Life Plan

Have you ever sat down to work on a very important project and you realize that you have to clean the space around your work area? This is a common experience. As we move into our Inspired Purpose, we become more sensitive to our surroundings. We are more affected by the energy of the 'stuff' in our space.

We also may not live in the ideal situation. This does not mean that we have to delay our work. It does help to get clear about what would support us to be or most powerful and productive. Often if we just state what we desire, the universe will find ways to make it happen.

To get started, find some time when you can sit quietly and feel into your daily life. If you can do this in the space where you spend most of your time, that is ideal. In that space, you can sit and evaluate what works for you and what doesn't work for you.

If the space where you spend most of your time is too busy or hectic, find a quite space in nature or elsewhere. Visualize your daily activities in your mind's eye. Think through how you spend your day and notice how it feels in your body. Do you feel joyful? Calm? Stressed? These are clues to your level of harmony or resonance with each activity.

Focus on those activities where you feel joyful, you are most likely in alignment with your Inspired Purpose. Think of how much time you would like to spend on those activities.

The next step is to create a list of your daily activities and list the physical conditions in which you carry out your daily activities. Then think about your desires, both short-term and long-term. Let's work through an example from my life.

Characteristics of Your Inspired Life

To begin my Inspired Life Plan, I sat on the porchof my house. Since I work from home, I was able to resonate with the energy of my workspace. I became quiet and felt into my daily activities, my short and long-term desires, and my physical surroundings.

Based on my feelings and what I knew I wanted, I made a list of the characteristics of My Inspired Life:

- My work inspires me every day.
- I live in a warm climate, surrounded bylots of trees and near my family.
- I work from my home 100%.
- I spend my work time as follows:
    - 50% writing
    - 25% speaking
    - 25% coaching or training
- My finances are secure – I have plenty of passive income.
- I have a partner or partners in my business and personal life.

Gap Analysis

"When it is obvious that goals cannot be reached, don't adjust the goals, adjust the action steps." – Confucius

Your Gap Analysis is a comparison between Your Inspired Life Plan and your current situation. It is designed to see where you can make changes and spend your time on different activities whenever possible. Here's my gap analysis.

- My work inspires me every day – Right now it's about 75%. My writing totally inspires me. Much of my data science work inspires me.
- I live in a warm climate, surrounded bylots of trees and near two of my children – *Yes.*
- I work from home 100% – *Yes.*
- I spend my work time as follows:
    - 50% writing – now only about 20%
    - 25% speaking – now only about 5%
    - 25% coaching or training – *now only about 5%*
- My finances are secure and I have plenty passive income – Plans are in place for 50% of my income to be passive income within 1 year.
- I have a partner or partners in my business and personal life – *Yes*

You can see by my Gap Analysis that I have some room for improvement. My daily practice is to read my plan each day and refine it when I receive more guidance or get new inspirations. And most importantly, since I have clearly stated my desires to the Universe, I pay close attention to what shows up in my life in response.

Seeding Our Inspired Purpose

Now that we have refined our Personal Values, created our Inspired Life Plan and performed our Gap Analysis, we have begun seeding our Inspired Purpose. Now let's explore steps we can take to further clarify and seed our Inspired Purpose.

As I've shared, I spent most of my early life feeling lost and directionless. One thing I have learned is that when I work towards goals that inspire me, everything seems to come easily and fall into place. Activities that were once challenging now feel effortless.

"You may be right. I may be crazy. But it may just be a lunatic you're looking for." – Billy Joel

One major concern I've struggled with over the years has been fear around my business reputation. If I came out preaching about love in business, people might think I was some sort of lunatic. As I felt into this fear, I realized that I wasn't loving myself and trusting my guidance. I decided to do some work about stepping into my power.

In my process, I realized that I had a great fear of stepping into my power and being annihilated. I used a process to remove old family and past-life trauma. I immediately felt a sense of freedom and fearlessness.

Now I feel inspired to become a champion for more love in the world. I try to be loving to everyone I meet. And my research into what drives business profits seemed to point in the same direction. It's all about love. So, I am finally declaring my Inspired Purpose:

"I want to inspire people to bring more loving behaviors into business in order to make the world a better place. I feel that if we can prove to leaders that loving behaviors, compassion, connection, and caring, will lead to higher profits, we can help leaders open their hearts, care for their employees, their customers, and the planet at large." – Olivia Parr-Rud

Writing this book is a huge step in this direction. Each day, I feel the joy of working towards my Inspired Purpose. I feel that if I stay focused on my Inspired Purpose, I will be supported by forces beyond my imagination.

The Power of Spiritual Practice

During my formative years, there was very little spiritual practice in my life. Like many families, we were just trying to survive. And as I've shared, my life was pretty chaotic.

During an occasional visit to my family church, I experienced some religious practices. But since my mother gave up on God after my father died, even attending church never felt sacred.

In many cultures, regular spiritual practice or ritual is very common. There is a huge body of research that shows how regular spiritual practice, whether done alone or shared with loving and supportive family and friends, can heal us both physically, emotionally, and spiritually. All of the Practices in Chapter 1 can be integrated into your personal Spiritual Practice.

In addition, you can create regular family traditions, coming of age ceremonies, rituals of friendship and community, commitment and separation ceremonies, seasonal celebrations, and celebrations of entering our golden years as Elders and Crones.

So, as I embraced my own spiritual journey and opened my mind to a wider range of spiritual influences, I experienced a growing hunger to bring more consistent spiritual practices into my life.

Given my commitment, you can imagine my excitement when I met Dr. Tererai Trent at the Emerging Women's Conference. As I read her inspiring book, "The Awakened Woman," I realized that my life struggles pale in comparison to the formidable challenges she overcame to realize her dreams.

From her roots in rural Zimbabwe where girls are minimally educated and often forced into marriage in their early teens, Tererai declared her dream.

It took her many years, but she achieved her dream of coming to America getting an undergraduate degree, a Master's Degree, and a PhD and returning to her native country to build schools for girls. If you have any excuse for not going for your dreams, I highly recommend reading her book.

I continue to be inspired by Tererai's story. Her determination and ability to handle adversity aretruly admirable. What surprised me the most was feeling envious of her as she shared the richness of her culture.

She was surrounded by a loving, supported family that believed in her and helped in numerous ways throughout her journey. She learned very early how to work with soil and grow food to nourish her community – something I hope to learn someday soon. And finally, she understands the power of spiritual practice, or ritual, at a very deep level. As I said, I am embracing this now.

Practices and Rituals for Seeding Your Dreams

I have several daily practices or rituals I perform to seed the manifestation of my Inspired Purpose. First, I spend time each day in mediation or contemplation. Sometimes, my mind remains empty. Other times, I get new insights and ideas for stepping into my Inspired Purpose.

Another of my seeding practices is reviewing and refining my Inspired Life Plan each day. During this time, I feel the energy of my Inspired Purpose being realized. Some spiritual teachers suggest that feeling into what you want to create is as or more powerful than just taking action.

An ongoing practice that feels powerful in my life is monitoring with whom I spend my time. I strive to spend my precious community time with like-spirited individuals. I've noticed that if I spend time with negative people, my energy is drained. If I spend time with positive people who are also on a spiritual path, my energy increases. For me, the balance of social time and alone time is critical for my well-being.

Tererai offers a powerful practice for "rootedness and planting your sacred dream seeds with the intention of grounding you in the face of busyness, adversity, fear, the common chaos in our modern lives, of inspiring you to remain on a clear path towards your true purpose." I offer a few excerpts below.

"This prayer offers much to you, but it also askes a lot of you: it asks you to spend some time in purposeful reflection on what needs to be healed and what longs to be manifested" writes Tererai.

She goes on to instruct us to "dig into the chambers of your heart, into the viscera and depths of your being. Search inside yourself for the place beyond fear where your dreams remain untapped." She invites us to delve further into our experience in many beautiful ways. Then she poses the question, "How will you turn the hunger in your heart into a practice for personal and communal recovery?"

Final Thoughts

Stepping into your Inspired Purpose can be scary. And it can be the most exciting, rewarding, and satisfying step in your life.

As I am taking this step, I suddenly feel the need for less material objects. I notice how amazing people who are aligned with my purpose are magically showing up in my life. And I feel so centered and peaceful as the world appears to be in chaos.

My sense is that once you decide to take this step, you receive support and experience a new level of joy. After all, this is what the universe is waiting for you to do.

Reflections

As you step into your Inspired Purpose, I invite you to revisit the Practices in Chapter 3. See if any would support you on a regular basis.

I also invite you to design your Inspired Life plan. Spend a few days refining it. Share it with close friends if you feel called to do so. Then make review and refinement of your Inspired Life Plan part of your daily practice.

And finally, I invite you to adopt some Spiritual Practices that feel resonant with your mission. Explore a variety of spiritual traditions that speak to you. And be open to new insights and ideas that may emerge as you tap into your deepest wisdom.

Chapter 6
Engage with Your Tribes

"A human being is part of a whole, called by us the 'Universe,' a part limited in time and space. He experiences himself, his thoughts and feelings, as something separated from the rest – a kind of optical delusion of his consciousness……... Our task must be to free ourselves from this prison by widening our circles of compassion to embrace all living creatures and the whole of nature in its beauty." –Albert Einstein

After all of our deep exploration and integration, we are ready to share our gifts with the world. In the physical world, our tribes might range from a small group of friends to an auditorium of fans to a global audience. In higher dimensions, we may consider our angels or guides as our tribes. In this chapter, we'll discuss strategies for engaging with all of our various tribes.

Finding Your Tribes

Our first tribe is usually our family. From birth until we start pre-school or enter daycare, our family gives us our earliest reflection of who we are. As we get a little older, we may find another tribe among our school or neighborhood friends.

Often, our expression during these early years may be very similar to how we desire to express ourselves now. If we are raised in a relatively safe environment, we often express our truest self while we still have our sense of innocence. However, early traumatic experiences can be the most difficult to understand and heal.

As a child, I seemed to be the neighborhood peacemaker. I could often see both sides of an argument. So, my friends would come to me to settle arguments. I think it my ability to see the big picture or think in systems that allowed me to make connections and bring understanding to both sides. And I always wanted everyone to get along. I guess that was my desire for us to all love each other.

Depending on your Inspired Goal, your tribe may be your coworkers or a small group of friends. Sometimes just sharing some of your fears and dreams with close friends is a powerful step towards fulfilling your Inspired Purpose. If your tribe is meant to be large, it will continue to expand as you step forward with your gifts. Just start with small groups.

As I shared earlier, I struggled to find my bearings in my first corporate job. As I shared more from an open-hearted space, I began experience deeper connections with certain people. I began to feel like I found a small tribe at work with whom I could be authentic. I had my richest conversations about spirituality with coworkers from other cultures.

"Community is intersecting circles of friends with similar interests and values."
– Stevie Ray McHugh

At this point in your life, your tribe is your community – the people in your life that share similar values and interests. I moved to Boulder, Colorado several years ago to meet people who are bringing spirituality into business. I felt that I truly found my tribe. I thought I would never leave. Even though I no longer live there, I will always consider Boulder my spiritual home. Eventually my guidance took me to Southern California.

Your tribe may be in your area. Or you may have to travel to connect with your tribe. I've attended several women's conferences lately where I've connected with amazing women whom I now consider part of my tribe. In many ways, my tribe now spans the globe.

Your life partner or soulmate is also considered a member of your tribe. Engaging in a deep loving relationship is a powerful way to discover areas of ourselves that are unhealed. My history of abandonments left me with a fear of deep connection. My relationships have been my greatest path of healing.

Tips for Finding Your Tribe

If you are the creative type, finding your tribe can be lots of fun. Here are some great tips to help you.

- Think of your interests or an activity you enjoy. Find or start a Meetup or some other group that focuses on your interest or activity. This works well for Social Media to find your virtual tribe.
- If you attend a party or social event, see if you meet someone where you feel a connection or you just feel good in their presence. Explore a deeper connection with that person.
- Get involved in volunteer work or offer to help others while doing something you love.

Andy Paige who works as a stylist on TLC, says that 1/3 of the people you meet will dislike you. 1/3 will be indifferent to you. The last 1/3 will love you. Don't worry about the 1st 2/3s.

Tools for Engagement

Presence Dialogue

"Thinking of the heart' is a much deeper and essential way of knowing then the ordinary surface mind can comprehend. The dialogue that ensues is of a different nature than an ordinary discussion. One not only listens without opinion. One "feels into another" picking up not just what they say but their "energetic signature," so to speak. One learns to listen with one's whole being."

– Joe Diamo, with permission, The Art of Presence Dialogue

A Presence Dialogue is a conversation that encourages us to open our hearts and speak from our heart. It can feel a little scary at first. But in my experience if it is done well and everyone feels safe, the resulting experience is rich and rewarding.

A Presence Dialogue typically starts with a meditation. This allows each participant to sink into their heart. During a Presence Dialogue there is no judging or debating. Each person is encouraged to share what comes up in the moment. If there is a facilitator, that person might help guide the conversation. The length of the dialogue and ending time is almost universally felt by the group.

If a group is interested in improving their process, they might share afterwards with a self-evaluation. I find this helpful when starting out in a new group.

Create a 'We-Space'

Once you enter into a state of Presence with others,
you create what some call a 'We-Space.'

> *"By welcoming all-of-you, the authentic sharing in 'We-Space' can be transformative. Perhaps it's because it lays down new neurons that are mirrored in the other participant's neural structure. These shifts may be barely perceptible in physical reality. But the good feeling of connection and mutuality with another human being invites love to permeate the space.* " – Antanas Vainius

The latest brain research offers fascinating insights into how we can leverage our connections. Based on the latest research in social neuroscience, as we feel empathy for someone else, we become attuned to their mood. The result is resonance. The two brains become attuned as if they are part of the same system. In addition to enabling rich connections with friends, this revelation has powerful implications for us as leaders, as it follows that truly "great leaders are those whose behavior powerfully leverages the system of brain interconnectedness."

Imagine the potential to healing and enhance a community's or team's ability to strategize, innovate, and more.

Secrets to Success

Have you ever felt so inspired that you had the energy of a three-year-old? When we are in flow with our Inspired Purpose, tons of creative energy are unleashed. This is the best time to start engaging with our tribe.

Now that we are ready to Engage with Your Tribe, there are some powerful, yet practical steps to help us improve our performance.

Make a Commitment

> *"Until one is committed, there is hesitancy, the chance to draw back, always ineffectiveness. Concerning all acts of initiative and creation, there is one elementary truth, the ignorance of which kills countless ideas and splendid plans: The moment one definitely commits oneself, then Providence moves too.*
> – *W.H. Murray*

I speak from experience when I say that the more committed, I became to my Inspired Purpose, the more opportunities, ideas, and resources began showing up.

The first time I caught a glimpse of my Inspired Purpose was way back in 1996 at my employer's quarterly meeting. The morning was full of business meetings. But in the afternoon, we were free to choose from a myriad of educational workshops. I saw a workshop called "How to Think Outside the Box" and knew that was for me. As I watched a very confident woman inspire a room full of bankers, I remember thinking, "I want to do what she's doing."

A few months later, I got an alumni letter from my college inviting graduates to present workshops at our reunion weekend. So, I decided to try my wings. I put together a 45-minute presentation called "Accepting Change and Moving On." It was a blend of exercises designed to help the attendees see what they want out of life. I invited them to consider where they might be stuck and why. I also included exercises to help them "Think Outside the Box."

To get some experience, I recruited my little tribe, my family and a couple friends, for a little evening of what at the time felt totally humiliating. My presentation was pretty awful. But I made it through and actually got some encouragement – and lots of suggestions. It was a tiny step but I went on to deliver a much better talk at my reunion weekend. It might seem like a minor event. But I feel it was significant because it was the first step towards stepping into my Inspired Purpose.

Set Goals

"Whatever you can do, or dream you can, begin it. Boldness has genius, power and magic in it. Begin it now." – W.H. Murray

On our journey to fulfilling our Inspired Purpose, we are most successful if we set small goals along the way. Many of us set high expectations and then get disappointed. This can be an unconscious way of validating our feelings of inadequacy. Others of us get impatient. We want to achieve great success without putting in the time or effort. Setting short and long- range goals can help us stay on track and gain clarity around our purpose.

After presenting at my college reunion, I set a goal of doing similar presentations at conferences. By 2004, I was regularly delivering talks and keynotes at major data conferences on the topics of Communication, Creativity, and Managing Change. I felt like I was living my Inspired Purpose. However, I wasn't able to make a living at it yet. I'm stepping into that phase now.

Focus on What's Right

When you feel that you are in flow, ask yourself questions like:

- What am I doing right?
- What is working well for me right now?
- Is there anything that would make it a little better?
- What resources do I need to make it better?

Avoid negative thoughts, questions, or judgments. Focusing on the negative attracts more negative energy to us.

This is a constant challenge for many of us. I work at staying positive every day. Following the practice of hanging around with positive people helps. And whenever you find yourself going negative, remember to be grateful for all the blessings in your life.

Tap Your Intuition

In Chapter 4, we learned that our intuition, accessed through the right-brain, is a better source of the truth than our analytic mind or left-brain. Our intuition gives us access to our highest and deepest wisdom.

Many of us struggle to access our intuition. So here are some simple techniques to help you build confidence.

Quiet Your Mind

It's helpful to have a question in mind or think of an issue with which you are struggling. That will help clear the chatter and allow your guidance to flow through. Also, have a notebook or some paper handy to capture any insights.

- Slow your left-brain by taking a few slow deep breaths. Put your attention on your breath. Visualize all the tension leaving your body.
- Start noticing any thoughts or insights that emerge. Your guidance can come through in many ways including a thought, an image, a feeling or even a sensation. Without any judgment, start writing about what is coming through.

I began honing my intuition many years ago. I was doing a lot of traveling. So, I often practiced in elevator lobbies. I would close my eyes and try to sense which elevator was going to show up. After a few years, I was correct about 98% of the time.

Practice Kinesiology

Another great technique for accessing your higher guidance or intuition is muscle-testing or kinesiology. It works by measuring strength in your energy body when something you think or say is true.

I first learned about this technique while reading a very insightful book, "Power Versus Force" by David Hawkins. This technique was reinforced when I learned the CLEAR® method mentioned in Chapter
3. Kinesiology works best when making true/false statements. See the Resources section of the Appendix for a link to full instructions.

One particular day, I was meeting a friend for lunch. The plan was to meet at noon. So, I figured I had a little extra time to run an errand. I muscle-tested the statement "I have time to run an errand.' I got a 'true.'

I left immediately and stopped for my errand. I figured I was going to make it on time until I hit terrible traffic. As a result, I was 15 minutes late. I thought my muscle test had failed. Then I saw my friend arriving at the same time. So, I did have time to run the errand and not make my friend late. If I had made the statement that I would arrive by noon, I probably would have gotten a 'false.'

Ask for a Sign

If you have a burning question that you can't seemto answer, ask the Universe or your Higher Guidanceto give you a sign. Be sure to state that you want the sign to be so obvious that you have no doubt that it is the sign you requested.

Many years ago, I attended a conference where a therapist shared an interesting story. He had a female patient who had no sense of self-worth. The therapist told her to ask the Universe for a sign that she had value. She left with a promise to follow his instructions.

The next time the therapist saw this patient she was radiant. She described her experience. As instructed, she asked the Universe to give her a sign that shehad value.

Later that day, she was driving with her windows down. All of a sudden, a bald eagle flew into her car, landed on her dashboard and looked her straight in the eyes. Then he flew out.

She said she felt totally different. She had received the sign she needed. I find it hard to imagine a more dramatic message than that!

Signs can also show up as synchronicities without even asking. I often notice patterns on the clock. One day I noticed the time was 1:11. The next time I looked it was 2:22. And the next time it was 3:33. I smiled and felt my guidance was telling me I was in sync with my higher guidance.

Learn from Your Challenges

Challenges show up when we are out of alignment with our Inspired Purpose. The depth of our reaction guides us to repeating earlier steps of the **LOVE@WORK** Method. If we are devastated by what we consider a failure or are judging ourselves as deficient, we may be reinforcing negativeperceptions of ourselves. If we are gentle with ourselves, we can move more quickly in a positive direction. We always have a choice about how we perceive ourselves. It serves us best if we focus on the positive. That allows us to being out the best in ourselves and others. If we feel incapable of seeing ourselves in a positive light, then we most likely need to go back to Step 1 and practice more self-love.

If our failure merely feels like a misalignment in our action, we may need to revisit our Superpowers or reassess our Inspired Purpose. And don't be afraid to ask for help. We are not here to do it alone.

Learn from Your Successes

When we are on a roll, we can learn from our successes. Think about when you felt satisfied with your performance. What were the conditions? How did you feel physically? What did you do to prepare?

Do you notice any patterns? Did you celebrate your success? Where there any negative behaviors that you avoided? Especially pay attention to your emotions. They are a guide to your success patterns. And they allow you to tap into your intuition – which is almost always available when you experience success.

Feel Fear and Act

"Vulnerability is the birthplace of love, belonging, joy, courage, empathy, and creativity. It is the source of hope, empathy, accountability, and authenticity. If we want greater clarity in our purpose or deeper and more meaningful spiritual lives, vulnerability is the path." – Brené Brown

To take a stand for bringing love into the workplace and living an inspired life, sometimes I need every ounce of courage I can muster. There are times when I feel very vulnerable. This is where I always experience my greatest growth. I no longer worry about failing. I know it's a very important part of the journey. I have so many battle wounds. Failure has been my greatest teacher. And gratitude has been my greatest healer.

Healing with my Tribe

As my Inspired Purpose began to reveal itself to me, I sought out opportunities to gain leadership skills. In early 2005, I was invited to attend a 10-day leadership training called The Temagami Experience. I knew and trusted the facilitators. So, I felt this would be a powerful experience. Little did I know that it would present one of the deepest opportunities to love all of myself.

In early August 2005, I arrived on a remote island in the middle of Lake Temagami in northern Canada. I, along with nineteen other participants and four leaders, became immersed in a series of individual and group processes designed to facilitate healing and self-realization. The week was filled with many terrifying and wonderful experiences that combined the best of traditional management training with Eastern spirituality and Native American ritual. The activities included a ropescourse, several sweat lodges, group gestalt work and a three-day vision quest. I moved through many levels of emotional and spiritual opening that allowed me to emerge in a state of fearlessness and deep reflection.

On the final evening, we each had an opportunity to engage with the group. We were invited to design our own healing experience that the group was invited to witness. They asked us to think of what most terrified us… As I think back, I'm reminded a few lines of a poem by J. Foster.

"You never knew you had so much courage. The courage to wake every morning. To take each new breath. To feel each new serge of joy, doubt, frustration, anger, pain, ecstasy, moment by moment, broadcast in real time, on the screen of life."

During the planning, I sought help. I wanted to take advantage of this loving group to work through my deepest fear. J Foster continues:

"To never settle for less than life, less than what it's worth, because it's worth everything, everything that's worth giving. And to have the courage to rise again. And breathe again. And dress again. And meet the new day-alive, curious, willing even though you are without defenses. You never knew you had so much courage." – J Foster

Somehow, I pushed through my fear and had a profound experience of self-love. To this day, I feel so much love and gratitude for my tribe holding space and witnessing my healing.

Final Thoughts

With so many ways to share your gifts, this is where the fun begins! The way I look at it, if I am engaging with my tribe in ways that align with my Inspired Purpose, how can there be anything to fear? Either I will enjoy success beyond my wildest dreams or I will discover more areas where I still need healing and self-exploration. And most of all, trust the process.

Reflections

Your tribe offers such rich opportunities for you to share your gifts and step into your Inspired Purpose. I invite you to let your imagination go wild. Feel into what might be the biggest expression of your Soul Purpose. Then consider a tiny step you can take. Set up a little event with your tribe. Experiment with sharing your ideas.

Taking that first step just to build the muscle. Don't worry about how well you do. Your friends love you for who you are – not how well you perform…

As you are taking your first steps, start honing your intuition. Also, I invite you to set some short and long-term goals. And celebrate even the smallest efforts. That will signal the Universe to bring you more of the same!

PART III
Love in Action

Now that you are on your path to living into your Inspired Purpose and serving the world, I'd love to share some powerful principles and practices that have profoundly enhanced my ability to thrive in my personal life and my corporate career.

I'm always inspired by principles and practices that seem so simple in concept, yet they can take a lifetime to master. As you read through them, you'll notice a lot of similarities. My sense is that these similarities reveal their deeper underlying truths. Enjoy!

Chapter 7
Loving Wisdom

"Coincidence is God's way of remaining anonymous"
– Albert Einstein

For thousands of years, wisdom has been gleaned from traditions all around the globe. In this chapter, I share some of the most powerful teachings and healing practices that bring my life into balance and fill my life with more love and joy.

Self-Mastery

Have you ever had one of those moments when you say something hurtful to someone and a little voice in your head says, "I can't believe I just said that." Or you can't seem to stop a destructive behavior, like eating junk food, even though you know it is not good for you?

I've done these behaviors more times than I'd like to admit... Here's what I've learned – rather than beating yourself up, these are times when you must love yourself even more – especially those parts of yourself that you wish were different. I know it sounds simple. It is not always easy.

Experts say that 95% of our behaviors are driven by our unconscious mind. To master our thoughts and actions, we be mindful of what is guiding our behavior in every moment.

I think this poem is an elegant metaphor for our lives as we strive to master our thoughts and actions.

Autobiography in Five Chapters
By Portia Nelson

I
I walk down the street.
There is a deep hole in the sidewalk I fall in.
I am lost...
I am hopeless.
It isn't my fault.
It takes forever to find a way out.

II
I walk down the same street.
There is a deep hole in the sidewalk.
I pretend I don't see it.
I fall in again.
I can't believe I'm in the same place.
But it isn't my fault.
It still takes a long time to get out.

III
I walk down the same street.
There is a deep hole in the sidewalk.
I see it is there.
I still fall in... it's a habit
My eyes are open; I know where I am; It is my fault.
I get out immediately.

IV
I walk down the same street.
There is a deep hole in the sidewalk.
I walk around it.

V
I walk down another street.

From THERE'S A HOLE IN MY SIDEWALK: THE ROMANCE OF SELF-DISCOVERY by Portia Nelson. Copyright © 1993 by Portia Nelson. Reprinted with the permission of Beyond Words/Atria Books, a division of Simon & Schuster, Inc. All rights reserved.

When I first read this poem, I realized how much I was playing the role of the victim in my life. I knew I was blaming other for everything that went wrong. After years of spiritual searching, I became so clear that everything was here to teach me and I had a choice in how I experienced everything.

In order to get to the point where we are responsible for our actions and create our own reality, we have to learn to be our own witness.

Becoming the Witness

Have you ever had this experience? You're speaking to someone and you impulsively say something that you know you will regret. The difference is that this time you are aware you are saying it while you are saying it! You might even think, "I can't believe I am saying this!" But somehow you can't seem to stop yourself. If you're smart, you'll apologize and saythat you didn't mean it.

The beauty is, that if you have that awareness in the moment, you are fairly advanced along the path of mastering your thoughts and actions. Most of us have no idea what we are saying or its effect until we hear back from someone. And sadly, sometimes we never hear back from people. We just notice people avoiding us.

It can be challenging to master our thoughts and actions in every moment. Mastering our thoughts and actions says we always anticipate the effect my words will have on one or more other people. It may sound simple but is far from easy. Every time you react with an angry comment or say something that you later regret, you are in Level 1 of mastering your thoughts and actions.

Before we review the levels, consider the following questions:

- Do you ever say something that you later regret saying?
- Are you ever surprised by other people's negative reactions?

- Do you find that certain people avoid getting into conversations with you?

I know some of these scenarios sound extreme. But we must look at any and all clues until we are able to track our own ability to master our thoughts and actions. If we feel really brave, we can also ask others for feedback. Consider asking a close friend the following:

- When I am talking to you, do you ever feel annoyed or frustrated?
- Do I have behaviors or lack behaviors that you find irritating or seem self-destructive?

Our ability to master our thoughts and actions may vary depending on our level of confidence in any given situation. When you read through these Levels, think about different situations where you might be feeling more or less confident. This might inform how stressed or relaxed you are. We tend to more impulsive and less aware of our thoughts when we are under stress.

Think about how much of your time is currently spent at each ability to master your thoughts and actions.

I can share from personal experience that this was a hard lesson for me. For most of my life, my emotions were unavailable. I survived almost exclusively using my intellect. I sought out an education that honed my quantitative skills. And I worked for companies in high level positions solving complex problems. So, if a friend came to me and needed to share something painful, I was ready with a solution. In fact, I became that dreaded friend that always offered advice. This came from a deep-seeded need to be valued and an inability to feel empathy. As I think back, I'm sure I annoyed a lot of people.

Many years ago, I was traveling with two friends. At that stage in my life, I think my ego was fed by offering unsolicited advice. I'm sure I was over- bearing. A few days into the trip, one of my friends took me aside and said, 'You really need to stop giving advice all the time." I said "why? Don't people want solutions?" She, "No. Often they don't" So I asked her what to do if someone is complaining and I can see a clear solution. She said, "Ask that person if they want a suggestion." I thought this was brilliant. Butit wasn't easy. I had to work hard at taming myimpulse to fix everything. I had to be aware of that tendency and remember to wait and ask if they wanted a suggestion. It still isn't natural for me and I slip up sometimes.

One day my dear sister-in-law called me to catch up and share about a problem she was having. She was used to my habit of instantly offering solutions. So, before she started getting into her story she said, "Olivia, I don't want you to fix it. I just want you to listen!" I was shocked! For a couple of minutes, I wasn't sure what to do. My automatic reflex to offer a brilliant solution wasn't even allowed! I remember being confused. I was thinking, well then why talk about it?

I gathered up my self-control and began to listen intently. I had to bite my tongue several times to keep from blurting out a solution. Soon, I started to see how just letting her talk was calming for her. I started to realize that my impulse to offer solutions might actually hinder her ability to process and find her own solutions. It was a real wake-up call for me.

Today, I still have a strong urge to fix people's problems. It's how I make my living! So, it's hard wired. And I have become much better at asking if someone wants a suggestion before I give a solution. And sometimes, when I know it's not appreciated, I don't ask if they want a suggestion. I just stay quiet and let them share. I feel it is a gift to listen and just send love and light.

Levels of Self-Mastery

As you embark on your path to Self-Mastery, the first step is to determine your dominant level – the level at which you operate a majority of the time.

As you read through the Levels, you might notice that it isn't always a simple choice. Your level of Self- Mastery may vary depending on your situation. In other words, you might be in total control of your thoughts and actions when you are in certain places or with certain people – situations where you feel confident and safe. Other places or people maycause you to be more reactive. I'm always a little more reactive when I'm around family. Visiting family is one of the best ways for me to see where I need to do more of my own healing work.

Your level can even be affected by how you feel. I know that I am less in control of my actions and reactions when I have a headache or I am tired or hungry.

As you read through the Levels of Self-mastery and compare the behaviors to your own, notice if you find yourself at a certain level most of the time.

To assess your level or Levels, read each statement out loud. See if you agree or disagree. Notice any feelings or sensations in your body. See if you can feel a resonance with one of the Levels. Consider situations when you are not feeling your best. Notice if your behaviors are at a lower level.

Level 1: Statements

"I say and do everything without regard for the consequences."

"I have no idea how what I say or do effects other people."

"Sometimes people respond negatively to me or avoid me all together and I have no idea why."

I spent most of my early life at this level. My unconscious behavior wasn't all bad. But when it was, I'm sure I lost some friends.

Level 2: Statements

"I often say or do things that I later regret."

"When I notice when people reacting negatively to me, I think about what I just said or did."

"I often think to myself 'I can't believe I just said that' or 'I can't believe I just did that."

Level 3: Statements

"I often notice that I am saying or doing something *while* I am saying or doing it but still can't stop myself, even though I know I will regret it later."

Level 4: Statements

"I am often tempted to say or do things I will later regret and I am able to stop myself or change my behavior."

Level 5: Statements

"I am rarely tempted to say or do things I will later regret."

Did you feel a resonance with one or two Levels? Here are some suggestions for getting to the next level.

Strategies for Self-Mastery

Level 1: Strategies

If you are unaware of how your words or actions affect others and you really want to change, ask for feedback. If you feel up for it, ask your close friends to give you immediate feedback in a loving and compassionate way. If that is difficult, another method is to request that people in your tribe participate in a 360° Feedback – a process that provides structured anonymous feedback from people in all areas of your life. See the Resources section of the Appendix for more information.

As I shared earlier, I got some harsh feedback before I could stop myself from giving unsolicited advice. I am so grateful to those who had the courage to tell me and love me through it all. I now have friends who help me notice things I want to change.

Level 2: Strategies

If you catch yourself after you say or do something you regret, the good news is that your witness is coming online. Take a deep breath to regain your center. Forgive yourself and remind yourself that you are doing your best. Then apologize to the affected person or persons. If you feel comfortable, you can share that you don't like what happened, that you are working on changing, and that you would appreciate their understanding and compassion.

I remember being horrified and feeling physically ill when I linked my recent behavior to the experiences I was having with people.

What a sinking feeling… And it still happens occasionally. It can still take some time for me to get past the self-admonishment to the self-forgiveness. But I eventually make it most of the time. And I try to apologize if possible. It's not always easy. But I find that it often helps the relationship. I've been amazed at how gracious people can be when I apologize from a deep and sincere place.

Level 3: Strategies

If you catch yourself *while* saying or doing something you will regret, congratulations! Your witness is now working in real-time. Again, forgive yourself and remind yourself that you are doing your best. Then apologize to the affected person or persons. If you feel comfortable, you can share that you are not happy about what happened, that you are working on changing, and that you would appreciate their understanding and compassion.

Sometimes I laugh when I realize that my behaviorin the moment is regrettable. Usually I'm eating food I shouldn't eat. If I don't realize this until after I'm done (level 2), my body reminds me in the morning.

I still say things I regret but don't often catch myself while I'm saying them. I am working on getting better that that.

Level 4: Strategies

If you are able to catch yourself before saying or doing something you know you will later regret, then your witness is fully online. Congratulations! Celebrate this achievement! If you feel comfortable, share your successes with close friends. Sink into and feel the joy of this achievement. This reinforces the behavior and reminds your brain that the behaviors you resisted are no longer wanted or needed. Eventually they will disappear.

While it's rare, I actually manage to catch myself sometimes, especially when I'm interrupted while in a meeting or group. I take the interruption as a sign that perhaps I wasn't supposed to say what I was thinking. After reconsideration, I end up following through about half the time. In the end I feel much more intentional and effective.

Level 5: Strategies

If behaviors you might regret are no longer showing up then celebrate! Bask in the freedom of this level of Self-Mastery. If you want to grow from this level, spend time honing your intuition. With access to your higher guidance through your intuition, you can say or do anything without thinking and serve the highest good for everyone involved.

This is hard to for me to judge because it's the absence of something. What I have noticed is that I have fewer regrets overall. I see what I used to do that I don'tdo anymore. So, I know I'm progressing.

Guiding Principles

In this section, I share several sets of guiding principles for powerfully navigating life. All of these practices are elegant, simple, and powerful. However, owning and mastering them may take some effort. I encourage you to pick one to start and see how you can embrace its concepts and practices in your life.

The Four Agreements

There are few teachings that are as powerful as they are simple. "The Four Agreements" by Don Miguel Ruiz fall into that category.

Based on the wisdom of the Toltecs, The Four Agreements are a practical guide to personal freedom. If we simply lived by these agreements, I think most of our day-to-day problems would disappear. The Four Agreements provide a foundation for living in the present and creating the life we desire. In practice, they are simple but not necessarily easy.

Be Impeccable with Your Word

"Speak with integrity. Say only what you mean. Avoid using the word to speak against yourself or gossip about others. Use the power of your word in the direction of truth and love."

In business and in our lives, our Word is the single most valuable asset we have. When we tell the truth, we gain the trust of others. When we gossip or speak badly of ourselves or others, we diminish our reputation. If we speak with integrity and say what we mean, we will respect ourselves and earn respect of others.

Being impeccable with our Word is foundational to bringing more love into our work and lives.

Don't Take Anything Personally

"Nothing others do is because of you. What others say and do is a projection of their own reality, their own dream. When you are immune to the opinions and actions of others you won't be the victim of needless suffering."
– Don Miguel Ruiz

As simple as this sounds, it is probably one of the most difficult practices to master. How often do we react or get upset by the actions of others? It does, however, get easier with practice. We are basically rewiring our brains to default to a positive thought rather than a negative thought.

One day, a dear friend of mine who has a low opinion of himself, shared how angry he was about a recent experience. He said he walked by a group of young adults and they were looking at him and talking under their breath. He assumed they were criticizing him. I suggested that maybe they were talking about how cool he looked. He shrugged that off. But it is important to realized that when we really don't know, we have a choice in what we assume. As we begin to love ourselves more, we begin to see the world loving us as well.

Don't Make Assumptions

"Find the courage to ask questions and to express what you really want. Communicate with others as clearly as you can to avoid misunderstandings, sadness, and drama. With just this agreement, you can completely transform your life." – Don Miguel Ruiz

I would argue that most of our misery in life is a result of our assumptions. Just becoming aware of our assumptions is a major step in the right direction.

A great way to practice gaining clarity around your assumptions is to talk to someone with whom you have a disagreement. Ask them to set aside some time to have a deep conversation.

Then take each point of disagreement and explore what might be each of your underlying assumptions. There is often a simple misunderstanding that underlies the entire disagreement.

Always Do Your Best

"Your best is going to change from moment to moment; it will be different when you are healthy as opposed to sick. Under any circumstance, simply do your best, and you will avoid self- judgement, self-abuse, and regret."
– Don Miguel Ruiz

We all know when we are making the effort to do our best. As we start to show up for our Inspired Purpose, it gets easier. I feel that when I do my best, I can feel good about any outcome. I feel that if we are truly doing our best, we can all give ourselves credit for our efforts and resist judging where we fall short. In my experience, this gets easier as we step into our Inspired Purpose because of the inner drive to keep moving forward, regardless of the outcome.

Ho'oponopono – Four Simple Steps

I love Ho'oponopono because it is a simple, yet elegant way to build four powerful practices into your life. Ho'oponopono is based on the concept that we are responsible for everything that happens to us, both good and bad. In other words, we can't blame anyone or anything for our happiness or our misery. This is not to say that we consciously cause ourselves misery. Most of our negative experiences can be caused by our unconscious thoughts and beliefs.

Using the four simple steps of repentance, forgiveness, gratitude, and love, Ho'oponopono has the power to heal our wounds and our perceptions of our experiences in the world. The order of the steps is not important. You don't even need to believe what you are saying. Just feel the emotion.

You can say the words silently in your mind. *"The power is in the feeling and in the willingness of the Universe to forgive and love."*

Step 1: Repentance – I'M SORRY

This first step is often the most challenging, especially if mistakes were not tolerated in our family of origin. If we were punished for making a mistake, saying "I'm sorry" can feel very scary.

I invite you to start with small stuff. You bump into someone. You drop something. Look for little things that allow you to practice.

If you feel ease with the little stuff, think about what's wrong with the world. Given that we are all connect, we can apologize for our part in pollution, or war. This doesn't mean that we are directly at fault. Just the act of saying "I'm sorry" can shift the energy and make a positive difference.

Step 2: Ask Forgiveness – PLEASE FORGIVE ME

Asking for forgiveness comes naturally after "I'm sorry." So just think of them as a sequence. Don't worry about who you are asking. Just repeat the words "Please forgive me." I think you'll be amazed as how freeing it can feel.

Step 3: Gratitude – THANK YOU

Saying "Thank you" is a powerful mantra in its own right. As a follow-up for repentance, it is even more powerful. If you feel like you are powerless when asking for forgiveness, expressing gratitude is a way of taking your power back. You are choosing the graciously accept your role in any situation.

I invite you to say "Thank you" often. I am grateful every day for my health and abilities to navigate the world. I make a point to thank my body, my mind, and all my support systems on a regular basis.

Step 4: Love – I LOVE YOU

We already know the power of love in so many ways. Saying "I love you" to everyone and everything is a way of really stepping into your power. In fact, I invite you to love your enemies! It doesn't mean that you condone what they have done. However, it can shift the energy in ways that potentially change their behavior.

Try this practice for a few weeks. Pay attention to subtle shifts in your experience.

Final Thoughts

We are blessed with so many simple and powerful principles and practices to transform our lives and our world. I invite you to build these into your daily lives. Print them on a small piece of paper and put them in your wallet or pocket. Refer to them until they feel natural. This is when automatic. Then watch for miracles to show up in your life!

Reflections

The greatest gift you can give yourself is to achieve Self-Mastery. It can be the single most powerful skill for taking control of your life.

Consider making The Four Agreements and Ho'oponopono part of your daily practice. Share them with others and ask them to remind you. Enjoy the beautiful relations that blossom as a result.

Love Always

It's been my pleasure to share this journey with you. Although it may feel like an ending, I invite you to think of it as a new beginning.

If you feel inspired to bring love into your work and life then remember – the world desperately needs you. You are that important! Future generations are calling on all of us to step into our greatness, share our gifts, and transform our world with love.

If you are one of the courageous souls who feels called to bring love into the corporate world, know that you are so valued and appreciated by those of us who want the corporate world to wake up, find its soul, and embrace a culture of love. Just imagine the healing that would unleash!

The corporate world can be a harsh environment, especially if you are a sensitive and open-hearted soul. I feel that by following the steps laid out in the LOVE@WORK Method™ you will discover the strength, internal calm, and resiliency needed to withstand and even transform the harshness.

As revealed in Chapter 2, our consciousness is continuously evolving. Our brains are evolving to handle more complexity and compassion. This trend suggests that each day there are more of us ready to embrace this new way of being in the world.

If you start opening your heart and share from a place of vulnerability and authenticity, you might be surprised at who shows up and resonates with you. Many people will drop their guard and relate to you more authenticity – your coworkers, you manager, you clients, you family, everyone!

"True power is the ability to relinquish control." —Olivia Parr-Rud

As we open our hearts and embrace love, we may feel like we are losing control. Our ego feels threatened because we haven't learned to trust our heart. As we heal and allow ourselves to be vulnerable, this gets easier. The ego or thinking mind finds itself in a supporting role.

If you want to make a positive difference in the world, then you must think of yourself as a leader. We must all think of ourselves as leaders – regardless of our position. As technology drives up the level of complexity, each of us can play a role in transforming our teams and tribes into more connected, compassionate and loving communities.

Essentially it all comes down to basics: love, trust, caring, compassion, etc. Even quantum physics is proving that we have to connect and care to thrive in our new high-tech, global economy. Lucky for all of us, the skills needed are good for humanity. I invite you to show up, open your heart, and lead fearlessly as we transform the corporate culture from a culture of fear to a culture of love.

Appendices

Appendix A – Resources

Applied Kinesiology

http://www.holistichealthtools.com/muscle.html

Equilibration

https://thankgodi.com/?s=equilibration

CLEAR®

https://www.changeworksinc.com/what-is-clear/

360° Feedback

https://www.hr-survey.com/360Feedback.htm

Appendix B – Chapter 2: Our Evolving Consciousness

Stages of Consciousness

Survival Archaic – Stage 1 [1st Tier]

Driven by an instinct to survive, the Survival or Archaic stage is characterized by an undifferentiated ego, sensory-motor activities, and a focus on short term safety. For the Individual, this stage ranges from birth to 1 year of age. At the societal level, this stage is seen in war zones and disaster areas and is roughly 250,000 years old.

Tribal – Stage 2 [1st Tier]

Driven by fear and a need for safety, the Tribal stage is characterized by magical beliefs, superstitions, and symbolism as well as impulsive behaviors. For the individual, this stage ranges from 2 to 5 years of age. At the societal level, this stage is represented in communities that are steeped in ritual and customs, and show respect for elders. This stage is believed to be about 50,000 years old and represent approximately 0.5% of the global population.

Egocentric – Stage 3 [1st Tier]

Driven by desire for individual power and instant gratification, the Egocentric stage is characterized by a strong drive which may include aggression and exploitation. At the individual level, this stage ranges from 6 to 11 years of age. At the societal level, this stage is often identified with rebellion against the tribe by individuals or through gangs and militias. This stage is believed to be about 10,000 years old and represent approximately 9% of global population.

Authoritarian/Traditional–Stage 4 [1st Tier]

Driven by desire for structure, discipline, sacrifice, and delayed gratification, the Authoritarian or Traditional stage is characterized by rules, roles, fundamentalist faith in God or Truth, and morality.

For the Individual, this stage ranges from 12 to 19 years of age. At the societal level, this stage displays behaviors such as the need to obey higher authority and rules to feel safe and understand the purpose of life. This stage is believed to be about 5,000 years old and represent approximately 30% of global population.

Enterprising/Modernist – Stage 5 [1st Tier]

Driven by desire to for individual achievement, logic, materialism, and independence, the Enterprising or Modernist stage is characterized by rationality, science, self-reliance, and behaviors such as challenges to authority and testing the limits of the system. For the Individual, this stage ranges from 20 to 39 years of age. At the Societal level, this stage presents as democracy, capitalism, and secularism. This stage is believed to be about 500 years old and represent approximately 40% of global population.

Humanistic/Post Modern – Stage 6 [1st Tier]

Driven by desire for peace, love, equality, and care for our environment, the Humanistic or Post-Modern stage is characterized by sensitivity, and a community focus. For the Individual, this stage ranges from 40 to 79 years of age – although as our consciousness evolves, this appears to be emerging at younger ages. At the Societal level, this stage is characterized by pluralism, civil rights, political progressives,feminism and environmentalism. This stage is believed to be about 100 years old and represent approximately 19% of global population.

Integrative/Emergent Integral – Stage 7 [2nd Tier]

Driven by a desire to balance the heart and the head, the Integrative or Emergent Integral stage is characterized by adaptability, autonomy, complexity, and the ability to take multiple perspectives and a systems view. For the individual, this stage begins at 80 years – although as our consciousness evolves, this appears to be emerging at younger ages. At the Societal level, this stage exhibits as members who are open and free and care for greater good. This stage is believed to be about 30 years old and represent approximately 1% of population.

Neo-Tribal/Mature Integral – Stage 8 [2nd Tier]

Driven by conscious evolution, spirituality, and self- actualization the Neo-Tribal or Mature Integral stage is characterized by taking a wholistic view of every situation. For the Individual, this stage begins at 80 years – although as our consciousness evolves, this appears to be emerging at younger ages. At the Societal level, members are co-creative, easily adaptable, and care for greater good while seeking to restore natural harmony and balance. This stage is believed to be about emerging now and represents approximately O.5% of population.

Transcendental – Stage 9 [2nd Tier]

Individuals at this stage are characterized by the essence of oneness while displaying wisdom and compassion. Their extra-sensory gifts and ego-less, non-dual nature are seen in saints and spiritual teachers.

As we explore these developmental stages, we notice some definite patterns. Each stage is more complex than the previous stage. Our evolution depends on the challenges we face and our willingness to move to the next level to solve the challenges. In that way, the increasing complexity compels us to evolve.

Also, the stages alternate from a focus on the individual (self-expression) to focus on the community or tribe (self-sacrifice).

As we experience more complexity in our lives, we evolve to higher stages to manage that increased complexity. However, we may have to revert to an earlier stage if required.

As we imagine ourselves evolving through the stages, I feel we can be hopeful about our future.

Barrett Seven Levels of Consciousness

Level 1

Individual: Foundations for Survival – At this level, we are concerned with our basic safety, financial security, and our health. People at this level make good financial managers who promote compliance. They are good in crisis management.

Organizational: Financial Stability – A company at this level is concerned with shareholder value as well as their employee's basic health and safety. However, their main focus is typically focused on profits.

Level2

Individual: Relationships & Connectivity – At this level, we value relationships with family and friends with a focus on loyalty and tradition. We value respect, recognition, and good communication.

Organizational: Employee Recognition – A company at this level put effort into good communication with and recognition of employees. They emphasize loyalty and fairness. They are concerned with customer satisfaction.

Level 3

Individual: Self Esteem & Performance – At this level, we begin to focus on our professional growth and skill development. We value success, quality, productivity, reliability, and accuracy.

Organizational: High Performance – A company at this level seeks out best practices that are used to build quality systems and processes.

Level 4

Individual: Learning & Continuous Improvement – At this level, we care about personal growth and seek knowledge so we can have the courage to take more risks. We care about work/life balance.

At work, we lead by building consensus and empowering our employees to take personalinitiative while holding them accountable.

Organizational: Continuous Renewal & Learning – A company at this level is mirrors our individual path with strong, agile teams that are empowered, goal oriented and accountable to the team.

Level 5

Individual: Alignment, Authenticity –At this level, we begin to sense that we have a purpose. We value trust, honestly, and commitment. We are usually more creative and have an enthusiasm for life.

Organizational: Building Internal Community – A company at this level has a clear vision and shared values that build trust and commitment. This culture creates openness and unleashes passion and creativity.

Level 6

Individual: Making a Difference / Collaboration & Partnerships – At this level, we are stepping into our role as a thought leader. We have developed our intuitive abilities. We have empathy for and are inclusive of others.

Organizational: Strategic Alliances & Partnerships – A company at this level is successful because of its ability to partner with others and care for its community and the environment. There is a focus on leadership development, coaching, mentoring, employee fulfilment, and community involvement.

Level 7

Individual: Service / Selfless Service – At this level, we are all about being in service to others and the greater good. We care about global peace, ethics, and human rights. We have the wisdom, humility, and compassion to forgive others.

Organizational: Service to Humanity & the Planet – A company at this level makes decisions and sets goals based on a long-term perspective. They care about future generations and embrace sustainability and social responsibility.

Theory of Social Maturity

Stage 0

As newborns, we do not have a developed sense of self. Absorbed in our own sensory experience, weare unable to distinguish the other. Our bodily actions are out of our control. If we are hungry or tired, we cry to get our needs met without any expectation who will respond. If we do not experience something directly, it does not exist. Around 18 months of age, we begin to differentiate ourselves from objects in our environment. That recognition pushes us to the next stage.

Stage 1

As we gain control over our reflexes, we gain a sense of independence from our environment. Our lives are rich with fantasy and our actions are mainly impulsive. We truly live in the present moment. As we mature, we begin to take responsibility for our behaviors and see the world more realistically. Mastery of these behaviors enters us into the next stage.

Stage 2

As we master our behaviors, our thinking becomes for logical and organized. Our daily routines take on more structure as we follow rules and directions. As we relate to others as unique individuals, we begin to classify objects, people, and ideas into categories. Our feelings are more enduring. We first experience competition and collaboration in peer group settings. As we take the needs and desires of others, we evolve to the next stage.

Stage 3

As we become more socialized, we are able to take an abstract view. We consider the feelings and processes of others in our family and community. Since we want to be accepted, we care about how we are perceived by others. The tension at this level is between our desire for autonomy and our desire for mutually nurturing relationships that minimize codependence

Stage 4

Our ability to perceive ourselves as part of a larger system gives us the opportunity for self-authorship. Rather than seeing ourselves as victims, we have the ability to take responsibility for and ownership of our own thoughts and actions thereby claiming internal authority. We begin to develop our own set of values and ideologies. Relationships evolve from being our primary focus to being a facet of our complex lives with opportunities for self and other as we gain clarity about our values and purpose.

Stage 5

Characterized by self-transformation, this stage is rarely reached and never reached before the age of 40. Our experience at this stage is characterized by recognizing the interdependence and connection of all people and systems at the global level. Relationships can be truly intimate and serve each partner to achieve their greatest potential. Although they are very rare, work environments are rare but once reached have the potential for great transformation on a large scale.

Engage with Olivia

Olivia works with individuals and groups who have the desire to take their growth to the next level and make a positive difference in the world. She specializes in working with people who want to bring their love and light into the corporate world through strength and vulnerability.

Olivia offers customized programs as well as individual and group coaching and webinars. Olivia is also available for speaking engagements and business consulting. Please visit www.oliviapr.com for a full list of offerings and the latest events and courses.

About Olivia

Olivia is a global thought leader, data scientist, and award-winning and best-selling author. Her unique approach to business success draws on her passion for data science, holistic leadership, and human potential through a blending of left-brain and right- brain models and practices. Her latest research unveils the relationship between employee engagement, loving behavior (i.e. compassion, connection, and caring), and long-term corporate profits.

Olivia has a BA in Mathematics, an MS in Statistics, and is a lifelong learner with a passion for systems theory, quantum physics, psychology, andspirituality. Clients include Cisco, Walmart, Wells Fargo, Fleet Bank, HBSC, Genentech, State Farm, Nationwide, Liberty Mutual, Clorox, HP, IBM, SAS, and Xerox.

Other books by Olivia

Data Mining Cookbook, Modeling for Acquisition, Risk and Customer Relationship Management (Wiley 2001). Written for data scientists, this highly technical book provides steps to build, validate, and implement statistical models using SAS® software. It is a global best-seller and is available in three languages.

Business Intelligence Success Factors, Aligning for Success in a Global Economy (Wiley/SAS, 2009). After spending years consulting for numerous companies in a variety of industries, Oliva saw the need to educate data- driven organizations on the value and power of their human capital. She spent years researching the financial and emotional benefits of effective communication, collaboration, and leadership in large organizations. This led to the unveiling of links between the global economy, organizational dynamics, and complexity science detailed in this ground-breaking book.

Business Analysis Using SAS® Enterprise Miner® and SAS® Enterprise Guide®, A Beginner's Guide won Best of Show at the Carolina Technical Book competition in 2014-2015. Written for data scientists who use SAS® software, this book details steps in building effective predictive models. Each chapter includes a section to help data scientists take their highly- technical results and effectively translate them for their business stakeholders.

Coming in February 2019: *The LOVE@WORK Method*™, *A Practice Guide* – takes LOVE@WOEK to a deeper level by offering insights, assessments, and exercises to help you live a life of inspired purpose.

Links and Connections for Olivia

Email Address: olivia@oliviapr.com
Phone Number: 215 948-3500
Website: www.LoveMakeItYourBusiness.com

Facebook Page:
https://www.facebook.com/LoveMakeItYourBusin ess/

LinkedIn Page:
https://www.linkedin.com/in/oliviagroup/

Twitter Handle: OliviaParrRud

Instagram: love.makeityourbusiness

YouTube: www.OliviaOnYouTube.com

Radio Show: www.quantumbusinessinsights.com

A portion of the profits go to The Oracle Institute
www.theoracleinstitute.org

Footnotes

1. https://en.wikipedia.org/wiki/Love
2. http://news.gallup.com/poll/165269/worldwide-employees-engaged-work.aspx
3. http://www.forbes.com/2009/06/23/employee-engagement-conant-leadership-managing- turnaround.html
4. http://www.sas.com/en_us/careers.html
5. Sandra Burud and Marie Tumolo, Leveraging the New Human Capital (Mountain View, Calif.: Davies-Black, 2004)
6. https://www.linkedin.com/pulse/love-new- currency-louis-carter?trk=v-feed&lipi=urn%3Ali%3Apage%3Ad_flagship_3_feed%3Br%2FUghWfjSYqfNbgSr7V64g% 3D%3D50
7. Ibid
8. Ibid
9. Ibid
10. https://en.wikipedia.org/wiki/Employee_eng agement
11. Raj Raj Sisodia, David Wolfe, and Jag Sheth, Firms of Endearment (Upper Saddle River, NJ.: Pearson Education, 2014)
12. Ibid
13. Ibid
14. Ibid
15. Kevin Roberts, Lovemarks, The Future Beyond Brands, Powerhouse Books, New York, 2004, p 49.
16. Tim Sanders, Love Is the Killer App: how to Win Business and Influence Friends, Crown Business, 2002.

17. http://www.fastcompany.com/3055657/mos t-creative-people/the-zappos-exodus-wasnt- about-holacracy-says-tony-hsieh?partner=rss

18. http://www.zappos.com/core-values

19. http://www.subaru.com/csr/diversity.html

20. https://www.subaru.com/csr/overview.html

21. Kevin Kelly, "What Technology Wants", Penguin Group, New York, 2010, p 270-271

22. Steve McIntosh, "Integral Consciousness, and the Future of Consciousness," Paragon House, 2007, p34.

23. https://www.forbes.com/sites/neilhowe/201 4/07/30/the-g-i-generation-and-the-triumph-of-the-squares-part-2-of-7/#359fd8ba29c8

24. https://www.forbes.com/sites/neilhowe/201 4/08/13/the-silent-generation-the-lucky-few-part-3-of-7/#f9e0a282c63b

25. https://www.forbes.com/sites/neilhowe/201 4/08/20/the-boom-generation-what-a-long- strange-trip-part-4-of-7/#18bf22661972

26. https://www.forbes.com/sites/nextavenue/2 016/09/13/the-undetected-influence-of- generation-x/#71bc0ad51efb

27. http://www.dailymail.co.uk/femail/article-4630930/Xennials-new-generation-born- 1977-1983.html

28. https://www.forbes.com/sites/shamahyder/ 2014/03/04/here-is-what-you-need-to-know-about-millennials/#7392c058311d

29. https://www.forbes.com/sites/robasghar/20 14/01/13/what-millennials-want-in-the- workplace-and-why-you-should-start-giving- it-to-them/#2864e3d64c40

30. https://www.forbes.com/sites/onmarketing/ 2013/05/28/generation-z-rebels-with-a-cause/#7f714ef69c28

31. http://bigthink.com/videos/three-technologies-that-changed-our-brains

32. New book coming on Neuroplacicity

33. Ibid p 72

34. Wendy Wallbridge, "Spiraling Upward, 5 Co- creative Processes for Women on the Rise" (Brookline, MA: Bibliomotion, 2015) p 10.

35. www.changeworksinc.com

36. Thomas Lewis, M.D., Fari Amini, M.D., & Richard Lannon, M.D., A General Theory of Love, (NY, NY: Random House, 2001)

37. http://www.selfgrowth.com/articles/being-a- witness-to-our-suffering

38. https://hbr.org/2001/02/when-to-trust- your-gut

39. Max Marmer, In Quest of Super Humanity In Quest of Super Humanity VIA CONSCIOUSNESS, BIOHACKING & ENTREPRENEURSHIP

40. http://www.maxmarmer.com/blog/super- humanity-resource-guide/

41. Ibid

42. Dr. Tererai Trent PhD, "The Awakened Woman," Enliven Atria, An Imprint of Simon & Schuster, (NY, NY, 2017) p 8.

43. https://www.suecimino.com/2018/03/09/en coded-like-a-seed/

44. https://www.suecimino.com/2018/03/20/a- message-from-the-ancient-ones-for-you/

45. Get reference www.thepassiontest.com

46. https://msb.franklincovey.com/inspired/fran klin

47. http://www.in2vortex.com/2018/06/26/17- seconds-abraham-hicks-law-of-attraction/

48. Dr. Tererai Trent, p 58.

49. Ibid p 59.

50. Ibid p 60.

51. http://www.marcandangel.com/2010/08/16 /how-to-build-your-tribe-finding-your- people/

52. Daniel Goleman and Richard Boyatzis, "Social Intelligence and the Biology of Leadership," Harvard Business Review 86, No. 9 (September, 2008 74–81.

53. Ibid., 76.

54. Don Miguel Ruiz, "The Four Agreements, A Toltec Wisdom Book," Amber-Allen Publishing, 1997 Inside Front Flap.

55. Ibid

56. Ibid

57. Ibid

58. http://www.laughteronlineuniversity.com/pra ctice-hooponopono-four-simple-steps/

59. Ibid

60. Gayle Van Gils, Happier at Work, Berkely, CA, She Writes Press, 2017, p93.

61. http://cgi.stanford.edu/~dept-ctl/tomprof/posting.php?ID=1110

Reviews

Linda Patten

Coming from the military and corporate, **LOVE@WORK** really spoke to me. Olivia challenges us to create cultures where more individuals, when asked, see themselves as leaders; and where leaders are truly valued for who they are not just what they bring to the table. Not only does she support her mission with research, but also gives us the "how-to's" to begin that work within ourselves. The story of her journey was real and raw, and gives me hope for myself as well as other leaders to carry on the work of changing and healing the world.

Linda F. Patten, Leadership Trainer for Women
Entrepreneurs and Changemakers – President &CEO,
Dare2Lead With Linda,
Website: www.dare2leadwithlinda.com,
email: linda@dare2leadwithlinda.com
website: www.dare2leadwithlinda.com
https://www.facebook.com/dare2leadwithlinda
https://www.facebook.com/linda.patten.311
https://twitter.com/patten_linda
https://www.linkedin.com/in/lindapatten

Dr. Ruth Anderson

Author Olivia Parr-Rud is a force to be reckoned with! I was fortunate to meet Ms. Parr-Rud in person and discuss her latest book, ***LOVE@WORK The Essential Guide to a Life of Inspired Purpose***. A prolific author in the genre of business, Parr-Rud branched out to incorporate the heart and soul of individuals in the workplace. The narrative is punctuated with many examples involving familiar businesses, which made for interesting reading. I found the author's dichotomy between being fluent in business practices while incorporating concepts such as deep breathing, meditation, gratitude, and forgiveness to be fascinating and welcome. The beautiful thing about Parr-Rud's recent work is that it appeals not only to those managing the worksite, but to anyone who has a heart and would like to make the worksite more humane, and love-filled. That's right, Parr-Rud calls on us to revitalize corporate culture in an attempt to meet the heart, soul, and needs of employees. Not surprising, the results of incorporating heart into existing business practices result in more profitability. ***LOVE@WORK*** serves as not just a call to action for individuals in business management, but provides a template for a life well lived, whether gainfully employed by anyone else or not. Corporate America would benefit greatly if ***LOVE@WORK*** were to become required reading for students in University Business programs.

Dr. Ruth Anderson
Founder, Enlightened World
ruth.anderson@enlightenedworld.online

Marian Head

Olivia Parr-Rud is what I call "Smheart." She effectively applies her brilliant, systems-oriented mind and her open, loving heart to the task of proving that Love is the greatest driver of success in business today. Inspiring us to love ourselves, others, and our work, she offers wise insights, illustrative personal experiences, and a variety of practical tools to guide us. Thank you, Olivia, for showing us the Why and the Way to **LOVE@WORK**.

Marian Head, author, Revolutionary Agreements: A Personal Path to Peace on Earth

Marian@RevolutionaryAgreements.com
303-995-3738
https://AgreementsInstitute.com
https://Facebook.com/MarianHead

David Newman

"If you're serious about building world-class organization, then you need to read **LOVE@WORK** right now. Insightful, forward-thinking, and immediately actionable, Olivia gives you the roadmap to the organization of the future - one where people, profit, and purpose converge into the X-factor of results, revenue, and marketplace success. Get a copy for everyone. Yes, it's that good."

David Newman, author of *Do It! Marketing*

David Newman, CSP
Do It! Marketing, Helping Professionals Market Smarter and Experts Speak More Profitably

p:(610) 716-5984 | e:david@doitmarketing.com |
w:http://www.doitmarketing.com

Rev. Laura M. George

"As a former attorney to the business community and as the current director of a spiritual community, I applaud Olivia for showing us the interconnectedness of *all* communities. Indeed, Love is the glue that holds everything together, and it is the key ingredient to all successful ventures. **LOVE@WORK** proves this point well. Using facts and figures, cutting-edge research, time-tested social theories, and Olivia's impressive experience in the corporate sector as well as examples from her life journey, she convincingly illustrates that **LOVE@WORK** benefits everyone – from shareholders to executives to front line workers. Moreover, it protects our planet from corporate waste which threatens all life. Let us embrace Olivia's holistic and prosperous business practices and co-create a culture of compassion at the workplace and *every* place!"

Rev. Laura M. George, J.D., Executive Director of The Oracle Institute and Oracle Institute Press, founder of the Valley of Light Community, and award-winning author of *The Truth: About the Five Primary Religions*, *The Love: Of the Fifth Spiritual Paradigm*, and *The Light: And the New Human*

www.TheOracleInstitute.org
www.PeacePentagon.net
www.OracleGuests.com

www.Facebook.com/OracleInstitute
www.YouTube.com/user/OracleInstitute

Sue Marchner Brightman

"Applause for Olivia Parr-Rud using her decades of background in the corporate world as a data and technical expert, keen observer of workforce performance and productivity, and critical thinker about the role of love in effective leadership. Where love has been deemed a soft and unrealistic commodity in the past toolkit of leaders, Olivia wisely challenges us to think differently about its powerful effect on employees — and ultimately on organizations' products and services. It takes courage to speak about love in business. Olivia's life and work proves to be courageous over and over again."

Sue Marchner Brightman

Founder, Brightman Glover International Coaching and Consulting in Conscious Business

President, For Women on the Journey of Their Lives

Author, forthcoming *Manifesta of Active Wisdom from 100 Women Over 50: A Call To Further Becoming*

Jeanne Alford

Adding "love" to the workplace is now a possible dream! Olivia presents a clear, concise approach to encourage significant growth in our lives and, thus, in our workplace. I found a kindred spirit in Olivia as she shared her story and the insights she gained along the way. The book is an easy read and provides great guidance, advice and tools to use. I really loved her focus on superpowers! One of those is choice. We can choose how we react to every situation. In ***LOVE@WORK***, Olivia shows us how we can choose to be strong, inspired and effective.

Jeanne Alford

Executive Coach, Media and Communications
www.alfordcommunications.com
www.beclear101.com

Mary Elizabeth Milbrand

LOVE@WORK is an integrative and holistic pivot within corporate America that showcases how a world that works is not only possible – it is essential. In businesses that include a vision for shareholders, employees, customers, and the earth, we are seeing quantifiable profits & overwhelming customer satisfaction! Olivia has tapped into a new era of capitalism with ***LOVE@WORK*** – where the conscious survive and thrive in this vocational paradigm shift.

Mary Elizabeth Milbrand, Designer and Visionary
@HeyMaryElizabeth {instagram}
youtube.com/heymaryelizabeth

Kathleen Neville

In her breakthrough book ***LOVE@WORK: The Essential Guide to a Life of Inspired Purpose*** Olivia Parr-Rud kindly shows us why we must truly be the 'author of our own life.' In sharing her deeply personal story and keen understanding of human nature, she expertly guides us toward a path that encourages us to be the most authentic version of our best selves. Through self-examination and honest reflection, she helps us understand how past experiences in our life, regardless of how difficult and painful they may have been, can ultimately lead us to our true calling; a life of inspired purpose. **LOVE@WORK** does not make light of the concept of love but rather points out how essential the presence of love is in all that we do, particularly and especially in our work and how we serve others. Before you once again ask yourself the deeply personal question 'what is my purpose on this earth?' you must read **LOVE@WORK.**

Kathleen Neville - author of *Good as Gold: In Pursuit of an Impeccable Reputation, Internal Affairs and Corporate Attractions*

Stevie Ray McHugh

Olivia Parr-Rud's groundbreaking book, LOVE@WORK, brings head and heart, hard data and intuition, practicality and humanity together to transform management practices from "profit first" to "people first."

Parr-Rud describes in very clear, well researched examples how a workplace that puts people's human development first grows past the profitability of companies just focused on the short- term bottom line.

Beyond management, she lays out a profoundly simple and effective path for employees who want to create a workplace based on respect, deep appreciation and, yes, love. With practical exercises, deep wisdom and profound understanding, Parr-Rud shows how to shift corporate culture for the betterment of people, planet and profits

Stevie Ray McHugh

Email: SR@StevieRayMcHugh.com

Marlene Elizabeth

Is your work environment driven by fear or love? Can love in the workplace increase profits? Are there financial benefits directly related to love-leadership? Olivia Parr-Rud's exciting book **LOVE@WORK** provides inspiring answers and intriguing data which powerfully supports her message that "love is the greatest driver of success in business today." Olivia brilliantly leads readers on a captivating journey inside "companies rooted in trust, caring and authenticity". You'll also learn how to uncover your inspired purpose, powerful secrets to success, excellent tips for creating an inspired life plan, plus strategies for healing trauma and negative patterns. Love this book!!

Certified Money Coach® and Bestselling Author of MONEYWINGS™

Website: www.GrowMoneywings.com Email: Marlene@MarleneElizabeth.com
Facebook: https://www.facebook.com/growmoneywings/

Maureen Metcalf

"The rate of technology change will continue to accelerate. Change requires business leaders to update their leadership "operating system". We need to identify the leverage points that will allow them to run thriving businesses well into the future. These changes are not one-time "fixes". We need to update ourselves, our cultures and our organizational systems. **LOVE@WORK** does just that. By updating who we are as leaders and how our organizations operate – by integrating love into the fabric, we transform our organizations and our experience of working in these organizations. When implemented, **LOVE@WORK** totally changes the world of work!"

Maureen Metcalf Metcalf & Associates, Inc.

Cell: 614.893.4532
www.metcalf-associates.com
CEO/Founder Innovative Leadership Institute
Regular Forbes Leadership Contributor
International Radio Host: Innovative Leaders Driving Thriving Organizations Tues 11 am PST
Author: Innovative Leadership Fieldbook (Integral Publishers) & workbook series
International Book Award Winner

Cynthia Stott

Olivia Parr-Rud has a fresh perspective on leadership and ***LOVE@WORK*** takes Servant Leadership to a whole other level. In this fast-paced global world, it's easy to go into fear, overwhelm and confusion. This book is a roadmap for transforming a business culture from fear-based to love-based, that ends in happier employees and customers and a bigger, more solid, bottom line. If you want to own your superpowers in business, then this book is for you.

Cynthia Stott, International Speaker Coach/Global Visibility

Influencer www.CynthiaStott.com
Programs@CynthiaStott.com
415.298.7306

John Castagnini

"In reading Olivia's book, you can't help but tap into the heart and soul of a leader who shares her genius on how to evolve a more loving conscious planet."

John Castagnini, Best Selling Author and CEO

www.thankgodi.com

44405833R00080

Made in the USA
Middletown, DE
07 May 2019